WINCHESTER ILLUSTRATED

The City's Heritage in Prints and Drawings

WINCHESTER ILLUSTRATED

The City's Heritage in Prints and Drawings

Alan W. Ball

HALSGROVE

First published in Great Britain in 1999

British Library Cataloguing in Publication Data

A CIP record for this book is available from the British Library

ISBN 1 84114 024 4

HALSGROVE
Halsgrove House
Lower Moor Way
Tiverton EX16 6SS
Tel: 01884 243242
Fax: 01884 243325

Printed in Great Britain by WBC Ltd, Bridgend

CONTENTS

Foreword by Mark Oaten MP   6

General Introduction   7

Distant Views   9

The City Centre   16

The Cathedral   46

Episcopal Palaces and Foundations   91

Other Churches   108

Winchester College   116

St Cross   151

Acknowledgements   175

Suggestions for Further Reading   176

FOREWORD

MARK OATEN MP FOR WINCHESTER

S et amidst the gentle rolling countryside along the banks of the River Itchen is Winchester, the capital city of Alfred, King of Wessex (849 - 899), who, after he had made it safe from the invader, began the books - the learning for his people. At the east end of the High Street stands a statue of the king, erected in 1901 to commemorate the thousandth anniversary of his death.

The Benedictine Order continued Alfred's work in pursuit of learning, and onwards from the tenth century, the scriptorium and school of illumination at Winchester reached a very high peak of excellence. The Normans built the magnificent cathedral church whose endless nave leaves one breathless.

In Norman times Winchester was of unrivalled eminence; an important centre for pilgrims who paid tribute at the shrine of St Swithun before taking the road to Canterbury.

William of Wykeham, Bishop of Winchester and twice Chancellor of England, founded Winchester College, whose motto is manners makyth man in 1382, and past students have made many important contributions to the scheme of things for our country.

In Winchester the past is all around us and we live within its fabric and fmd ourselves part of it. Old and new living alongside each other, a necessary tension of a modern world. For all of us there is a constant reminder of our heritage and the need to preserve the past whilst building a filture which will last at least as long as the legacy handed down by those who have gone before us. This book pays tribute to the artists and engravers of the past whose work illustrates this text.

GENERAL INTRODUCTION

At first sight it seems strange that so few of the great watercolourists of the eighteenth and nineteenth centuries produced work on Winchester. Turner passed through in 1795 and left some tantalising outlines in his Isle of Wight sketch book. One was of the Westgate and a second of the Butter Cross, while a third was a wash drawing of the west front of the Cathedral, but they were never worked up into full scale paintings. The Butter Cross sketch was to form the basis of an engraving by J. Powell in 1800, but this appears to be the only one covering Winchester from Turner's prodigious output in this medium.

Sadly there is no equivalent of Constable's drawings and paintings of Salisbury, occasioned by his friendship with Archdeacon Fisher, or of de Wint's series of paintings of Lincoln. Equally, there is nothing similar to Girtin's, Cotman's or Hearne's views of Durham or those of Turner himself. Hearne did come to Winchester and only produced a view of St Cross for engraving in the *Antiquities of Great Britain*, while Prout's drawings of the same building resulted in eight minute engravings for the *Antiquarian and Topographical Cabinet*. Rooker made a painting of the Westgate, now in the Manchester City Art Gallery, but there appears to be nothing by Varley, Boys, Bonnington, Francia, Wyld or the Sandbys. The exception was Callow, who exhibited five Winchester views at the Royal Society of Painters in Watercolours between 1845 and 1906.

However, perhaps the reason for this lack of material is not hard to find. Artists are most often inspired by striking and prominent landscapes, but although Winchester has a magnificent Cathedral with the longest nave in Europe and sumptuous internal decoration and fittings, the whole town sits down in a hollow. Lincoln, Durham, Chartres and Laon are built on hills that rise abruptly from a surrounding plain, while Chartres itself can be seen for 20 miles across the cornfields of the Beauce and Ely for the same distance over the fertile farmlands of the Fens. They all have the distance and perspective that Winchester sorely lacks.

There is also another reason. Salisbury Cathedral has the tallest spire in England, while Canterbury, Lincoln, York and Durham Cathedrals have handsome towers and seem to thrust themselves towards the sky, whereas Winchester Cathedral with its low tower seems to crouch against the earth and from St Giles or St Catherine's Hill resembles nothing so much as a vast and extremely elegant barn. This was the opinion of Joseph Pennell and Daniel Defoe was as usual even less complimentary in his *Tour Through the Whole Island of Great Britain* in 1724. He remarked 'The outside of the church (ie Cathedral) is as plain and coarse, as if the founders had abhorred ornaments, or that William of Wykeham had been a Quaker, or at least a Quietist. There is neither statue or niche for a statue to be seen on all the outside; no carved work, no spires, towers, pinnacles, balustrades or anything, but mere walls, buttresses, windows and quoins, necessary to the support and order of the building: it has no steeple, but a short tower covered flat, as if the top of it had fallen down and it had ben covered in haste to keep the rain out, till they had time to build it up again'.

It is because of the dearth of original paintings that published prints and drawings from the late seventeenth century up to the period immediately following the First World War provide such a fascinating insight into the life of the City. I have not included photographs because there are separate studies in the medium and in any event the amount of non-photographic material is so great that concentrating on that alone has required considerable selectivity. At the same time this book makes no claim to be a general history of the City, as an almost overwhelming amount of material exists already and I make brief reference to this in the section on Suggestions for Further Reading on page 176.

Many of the artists who produced work for engravers and lithographers remain elusive with little known about their lives and background. When their drawings appeared in books they were often regarded by authors as the providers of a little light icing on the otherwise substantial cake of their own deathless prose and the dismissive phrase 'from an old print' was felt sufficient captioning for an illustration. It is ironic that time has had a habit of consigning this literary effort to obscurity while the icing has achieved more sparkle and interest over the passing years.

It should be stressed however, that all this artistic effort rarely led to riches or even more than scraping a tolerable living. What would now be regarded as the highly sycophantic dedications of a number of prints was merely an attempt by artists and engravers and their publishers to drum up sales by associating themselves with the rich and powerful. This pre-occupation with knowing which side your bread is buttered should not obscure the fact that there is a wealth of very fine work in the pages that follow. In legal arguments the devil can be in the detail, but in prints and drawings the delight more often than not resides in the detail and for this reason I suggest the use of a magnifying glass can afford a great deal of enjoyment by bringing into sharp focus much that might otherwise not be noticed. As these prints and engravings often appear at a different size from the originals, I have indicated the real dimensions in millimetres with height first and width second.

Nor do they always appear in an orderly chronological sequence or one which is consistent in viewpoint. Artists are naturally influenced by the work of their predecessors, but thankfully are often also given to doing their own thing. However, the mixture of styles that follows creates a charm of its own, which I hope the reader will find intriguing in its own right.

Finally it should be made clear that there is such a wealth of available material that it has only been possible to include a carefully chosen selection and I can therefore only apologise in advance if many of your favourite illustrations do not appear.

A splendid piece of historical imagination showing King
Edgar being crowned King of the English at Winchester. The
dressed-up monkeys cavorting at the centre are especially
worthy of note and also the child and noble on the left looking
away from the main proceedings, no doubt wondering when
the feasting is to begin. This anonymous engraving forms the
frontispiece of Volume 3 of Robert Mudie's *Hampshire* of
1838 (136x110).

DISTANT VIEWS

It is significant that most of the distant views of Winchester are from the east, either from St Giles' Hill looking across the City towards St Catherine's Hill, from the latter straight across the City or lower down from the surrounding fields. St Giles' Hill is now built over with the M3 behind it further east, but St Catherine's Hill has been spared that indignity and is in fact owned by Winchester College, which has always used it as a recreation area. In the nineteenth century views of the City, buildings no longer existing, such as the Kings House by then used as a barracks, are clearly visible. The clump of trees which is such a feature of St Catherine's Hill was planted at the end of the eighteenth century by a company of the Gloucestershire Militia, that was camping there.

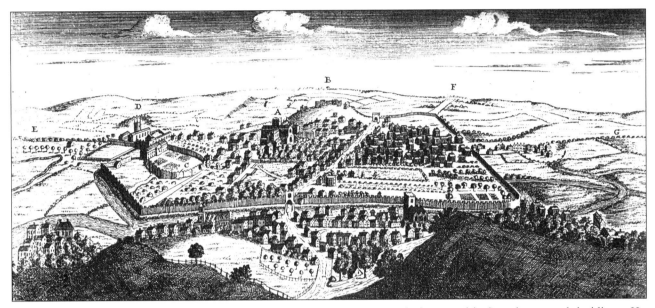

William Stukeley was an eighteenth century antiquarian who was extremely interested in Stonehenge and druidism. He was appointed Secretary to the Society of Antiquaries in 1717 and in 1724 published the *Itinerarium Curiosem*, which is as the title suggests, a rather rambling discourse on what he considered antiquarian curiosities. It includes this engraving entitled *Prospect of Winchester from the South*, which appears to be from the east, probably from St Giles' Hill and is dated 9 September 1723. It must be said that as an antiquarian Stukeley has a somewhat flawed reputation because he accepted Charles Bertram's forgery *De Situ Britanniae* as a genuine work by Richard of Cirencester and published it as such in 1757 (125x270).

This view appears in the 1796 edition of the *Winchester Guide* and is a straight piece of plagiarism, as it is an almost exact but very poor copy of the centre section of the engraving by the brothers Samuel and Nathaniel Buck of 1736. The artist and engraver is J. Ryland (100x176).

This anonymous undated steel engraving is entitled *Winchester from St Giles' Hill* and the publisher is T. Prouten of Winchester. The engravers are Norman and Barclay of London. The sheep in the foreground add a pleasing rural touch to the urban scene, but the third from the left looks curiously like a large cottage loaf (80x145).

A similar view to the one above. The artist of this finely detailed work is William Henry Bartlett and the engraver C. Cousen. It comes from Volume 1 of Bernard Bolingbroke Woodward's *General History of Hampshire* of 1861-1869 (125x200).

An anonymous wood engraving of Winchester from St Giles' Hill, that comes from the *Illustrated London News* of 13 September 1845. The woman in the foreground appears to be carrying a pile of sheets, which she has presumably just washed (160x240).

A section of another anonymous wood engraving from the *Illustrated London News* of 17 May 1873. This is also from St Giles' Hill and the boy flying his kite adds a slightly holiday air to an otherwise workaday scene (whole engraving 345x510, this section 345x210).

One of Herbert Marshall's sketches dated 1892 from *Winchester College 1393-1893* by Old Wykehamists, showing houses clustered round the east end of the Cathedral (145x200).

A drawing from rather watery fields to the east of the Cathedral looking towards St Catherine's Hill on the far left. But who is this rather mysterious woman in black bombazine and poke bonnet wandering through the long grass? The artist is Joseph Pennell and the wood engraver H.R. Sylvester. The view comes from *English Cathedrals* by Mrs Schuyler Van Renssalaer of 1887 (90x132).

Another of Joseph Pennell's drawings for Mrs Schuyler Van Renssalaer's *English Cathedrals* of 1887, with the wood engraving also by M.E. Sylvester. It is entitled 'Winchester from the Eastern Hills' and shows a very steep drop into the town from St Giles' Hill (195x135).

An engraving of the City and Cathedral from the north east at Winnall. The artist is W.B. Roberts and the view is included in *A City of Memories* by A.R. Bramston and A.C. Leroy of 1893 (100x150).

A sketch by Herbert Marshall dated 1893 *from Winchester College 1393-1893* by Old Wykehamists. It shows cricket being played by College boys on the Lavender Meads with the clump of trees on St Catherine's Hill prominent in the background (115x200).

An anonymous pencil sketch dated September 5 1903. It differs in angle from the one above, but shows St Catherine's Hill prominently. From the collections of the Society of Antiquaries (135x215).

An engraving looking from St Catherine's Hill towards Winchester. The artist is George Sidney Shepherd and the engraving from J. Shury and Son. The illustration comes from Volume 3 of Robert Mudie's *Hampshire* of 1838 and shows what appears to be a party of tourists talking to a rustic. One of them is looking at what is probably a guide book while herds and flocks are prominent in the background (115x150).

An engraving also from St Catherine's Hill which gives great emphasis to the River Itchen and its tributary waterways, but with herds and flocks still abounding and the Cathedral appearing distantly on the far right. The artist is William Henry Bartlett and the engraver S. Bradshaw of this work from Volume 1 of Bernard Bolingbroke Woodward's *General History of Hampshire* of 1861-1869 (130x210).

A sketch by Percy Robertson from the *Art Journal* of 1890 entitled the *Towers of Winchester*. The River Itchen flows peacefully through the foreground and a flock of birds rises above the central tower of the Cathedral (80x175).

Rock and Co.'s view no. 984 of Winchester from St Catherine's Hill, again with the River Itchen and its tributaries in the foreground and people strolling along pathways. A fisherman on the bank waits patiently with a companion for a bite (60x90).

Herbert Marshall's 1893 sketch entitled *View from the Hills* has a peaceful scene similar to that above. It comes from *Winchester College 1393-1893* by Old Wykehamists (150x200).

THE CITY CENTRE

One of the delights of wandering around a place you have never visited before, or with which you only have a nodding acquaintance is to notice the way that buildings of all dates blend together to form a pleasing whole or clash violently in teeth-baring contention. Although it is easy to deplore the loss of buildings from the past and dislike their often unloved replacements, it is as well to remember a city is a living organism which is constantly renewing itself. We should therefore be thankful that so much in a city like Winchester has actually survived.

The eighteenth century saw country towns acquiring a certain elegance with local magnates building or adapting houses in them where they could reside during a summer season, which mirrored on a small scale locally what happened in London and other big cities. Defensive walls and gateways were no longer needed and swept away as outmoded and barbarous. However there were voices being roused in antiquarian circles even at that date deploring the destruction of buildings. For example Robert Sayer in his 1774 re-issue of *Buck's Antiquities* writes: 'The design of the original publication (from 1726 onwards) was to rescue from the irresistible hand of time, and to convey to futurity those venerable piles of ancient Grandeur, crumbling to dust and hastening to their final dissolution, many of which are no more; having been since entirely demolished for modern structures, or perished by time or accident'.

In Winchester the irresistible hand of time removed four of the gates and the Westgate and Kingsgate no doubt only survived as the former was used as a debtors' prison and the latter is part of St Swithun's Church. It is recorded that the debtors had to feed themselves, an impossible task as they were of course penniless, so they had to resort to thrusting collecting boxes through the bars of their prison and throw themselves on the mercy of passers-by in order to survive. One of the reasons given for the destruction of the other gates was that they were an obstruction to the free movement of pedestrians and traffic, especially carts bringing hay to feed horses in the City, which had their loads greatly reduced in order to make the passage through the narrow and low openings. Nobody was in the business of finding ingenious solutions to this problem, so Southgate and Eastgate Streets, Friarsgate and North Walls are now the only reminders of most of the City's former defensive curtain.

The early fifteenth century Butter Cross, which is so much a feature of the High Street, was restored by Scott in 1865. However, it almost suffered the same fate as the gates, when unfeeling City fathers out to make a quick profit in 1770 sold it to a local landowner as so much useless stone, but the local citizenry rose up in wrath at this intended vandalism and chased away the demolition contractors, an early and spontaneous example of an instant conservation movement.

Winchester is notable for having the remains of two castles like the opposite ends of a dumbbell with the Cathedral between them. The first at the western end of the High Street was the work of William the Conqueror, as one of a number to secure his new kingdom. It was besieged by Prince Louis of France in 1216 and suffered grievously, but the subsequent rebuilding saw the creation of Henry III's Great Hall, the best example in the country after Westminster Hall, which was to witness the trial of Sir Walter Raleigh and the Bloody Assizes, presided over by the fearsome Judge Jeffries after the Battle of Sedgmoor. The attentions of Oliver Cromwell in the Civil War meant that nothing now remains of the Castle except the Great Hall itself.

The second is Wolvesey Castle built by Henry of Blois as the Bishop's Palace south east of the Cathedral and its close. It too had a great hall and suffered a siege at the time of the fighting between King Stephen and Matilda. After that date the Bishops of Winchester continued to live there as well as Farnham Castle until the Civil War when Wolvesey too was largely made ruinous. The present Bishop's residence of 1684 was considerably reduced in size by Bishop Brownlow North and replaced Farnham Castle when the latter passed to the new Diocese of Guildford in 1927 (see also pages 96 to 102).

One of the outstanding Winchester buildings, that was destroyed by fire in 1894, was a palace designed by Sir Christopher Wren for Charles II. Work was started in 1683, but was stopped in 1685 and in those two years a substantial building had emerged, which was later used as a barracks. After the 1894 fire a new barracks was constructed on the same site about 1900.

Among the other buildings not dealt with elsewhere the old and new Guildhalls are prominent features of the High Street. The former with its handsome bracket clock is now used for commercial purposes, while the latter of 1873 with a later extension has the air of a highly compressed French chateau. The County Hospital led a peripatetic existence in the eighteenth and nineteenth centuries from Colebrooke Street to Parchment Street before being settled on its present Romsey Road site in 1868. St John's Almshouses are a notable feature on Colebrooke Street and the only remaining part of the once great and extensive Hyde Abbey, the gateway, stands surrounded by later urban development north of the City's central core. On one occasion that noted Wykehamist, the Reverend Sidney Smith when Dean of St Paul's, startled a staid Victorian lady by saying 'Madam, it is so hot I am going to take off my flesh and sit in my bones' and this is what has happened to one of the City's oldest domestic buildings, the former rectory of St Peter's in Chesil Street, as it has had the original plaster work removed to expose the timber framing of its construction.

County Hall is outside the scope of this work, as it dates from the end of the 1950s, but the Stanmore Estate of the 1920s falls just within the time frame. Its architect was William Curtis Green, who was responsible for banks and insurance firms largely in the City of London and also the Dorchester Hotel. On the whole time and developers have dealt more gently with Winchester than many provincial towns since the Second World War and for that it can be profoundly thankful.

The Westgate is part of the original City defences and the upper section has been used at various times, as a prison, an annexe to a pub and a small museum. This view of the west face is by an anonymous engraver after a drawing of 1810 by Samuel Prout. From the *Proceedings of the Hampshire Field Club and Archaeological Society* of 1898 (120x160).

The east and west faces of the Westgate with detailing from the west face including keyhole gunports, two quatrefoils with shields and the remains of the machicolation. The drawings are by John Carter from his *Ancient Architecture of England* and dated 1789, with a publication date of 1 June 1802 (two elevations 120x90, two sections of detailing 140x70).

The artist of this view of the Westgate is William Henry Bartlett and the engraver Edward John Roberts. It comes from Volume 1 of Bernard Bolingbroke Woodward's *General History of Hampshire* of 1861-1869. Through the arch can be glimpsed the clock on the Old Guildhall and the Butter Cross with people going about their everyday affairs. The cart looks oddly like a Volkswagen Beetle bumping over one of the uneven road surfaces common at that date (180x120).

A rather martial scene with armed soldiers about to go through the Westgate. An anonymous wood engraving from the *Builder* of 9 April 1853 (170x135).

Owen Browne Carter's version of the Westgate engraved by John Le Keux. Who are the two curious figures approaching the arch? Are they Winchester College boys or pedlars carrying bundles of goods of some kind? In any event their headgear is certainly curious. From Carter's *Picturesque Memorials of Winchester* of 1830 (145x150).

A horse and cart near the Westgate. An undated but Edwardian drawing by Alexander Murray from the *Pilgrim's Way From Winchester to Canterbury* by Julie Cartwright. Although published later in book form this work started life as articles in the *Art Journal* of 1892 (140x100).

A drawing of the Westgate by Charles G. Harper from the Reverend A.G. L'Estrange's *Royal Winchester* of 1889 (103x72).

A view of the Westgate by Ernest C. Peixotto from *Scribners Magazine* January-June 1900, in an article on Oliver Cromwell by Theodore Roosevelt a year before his inauguration as President of the United States (75x85).

Artists were obviously more attracted by the martial west face of the Westgate and this much rarer view of the east face is by John Carter with James Basire as the engraver. It comes from John Milner's *History of Winchester* of 1809 and is almost an exact copy of Carter's drawing on page 17 with a similar date of 1789. Carter must have turned up his original drawing and just added the Castle Hall in the background (105x130).

A much later view of the east face of the Westgate with a vigorous growth of foliage at the top and a haycart on the roadway. It is by Alfred Rimmer in his *Ancient Streets and Homesteads of England* of 1889 (85x70).

The Kingsgate is mainly a fourteenth century structure with the church of St Swithun above and beside it (see page 114). The two pedestrians archways are eighteenth century. This sketch is by Herbert Marshall and comes from *Winchester College 1393-1893* by Old Wykehamists (125x105).

A painting of the Kingsgate and surrounding buildings by Wilfrid Williams Ball of 1907. It appears in the Reverend Telford Varley's *Hampshire* of 1909 (140x105).

A drawing of the Kingsgate by Charles G. Harper from the Reverend A.G. L'Estrange's *Royal Winchester* of 1889 (70x75).

The Kingsgate with Winchester College boys emerging from the shop on the right. The artist is W.B. Roberts and the drawing comes from A.R. Bramston and A.C. Leroy's *City of Memories* of 1893 (115x150).

A sketch by Herbert Marshall, also of 1893, looking through the arches of the Kingsgate down Kingsgate Street. It comes from *Winchester College 1393-1893* by Old Wykehamists (135x200).

Various views of the Butter Cross. At the left from *Vetusta Monumenta*, one of the publications of the Society of Antiquaries. The artist is Jacob Schnebbelie and the engraver James Basire. The date 'from a draught in the possession of William Draper Esq.' is 1741, but that of the engraving 1757 (465x305). Below left from A.R. Bramston and A.C. Leroy's *City of Memories* of 1893. The artist is W.B. Roberts (150x115). Below right from John Milner's *History of Winchester* of 1809. The artist is James Cave and the engraver J. Pass (160x60).

Further views of the Butter Cross. At the top left from Thomas Warton's *History and Antiquities of Winchester* of 1773. The artist is W. Cave and the engraver James Taylor (130x65). At the top right Rock and Co.'s engraving No. 1665 dated 1 July 1851 (85x60). At the bottom left a sketch by Jenny Wylie dated 1908 from Volume 5 of the *Victoria County History of Hampshire of 1912* (40x90). Below right an engraving by Owen Browne Carter from his *Picturesque Memorials of Winchester* of 1830 (210x175).

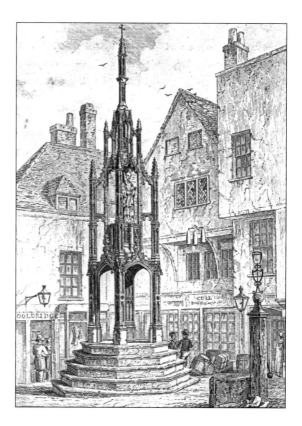

Three more views of the Butter Cross. At the left from Volume 1 of Bernard Bolingbroke Woodward's *General History of Hampshire* of 1861-1869. The artist is William Henry Bartlett and the engraver W. Wallis (175x135). At the centre right from *Ancient Stone Crosses of England* of 1875 by Alfred Rimmer, who is also the artist (140x90). Below left a painting by Wilfrid Williams Ball of 1907 from *Hampshire* by the Reverend Telford Varley of 1909 (135x115).

At the top a man with a stick and shopping basket, who has the air of an elderly verger, makes his way slowly past the Butter Cross. The artist is Herbert Railton and the sketch comes from *Our English Minsters* of 1893 edited by Frederic William Farrar, Dean of Canterbury, with the Winchester section by William Benham, who at that time was Rector of St Edmund the King, Lombard Street. Both men had trained under John Frederick Maurice at King's College London and Farrar, by one of those unfortunate quirks of fate, is now best remembered as being the author of the schoolboy novel *Eric or Little by Little* (133x85).

An academic and an ecclesiastical gentleman are deep in conversation near the Butter Cross and an idler lounges outside Tanner's shop. The artist is Joseph Pennell and the sketch comes from Mrs Schuyler Van Rensselaer's *English Cathedrals* of 1887. Pennell admitted that he 'was deadly afraid of her as she was an art critic'. He also loved to insert his own name in his sketches on shop fronts or advertisements and he has done this on the one above Tanner's shop, where he has transformed himself into the General Manager of the Great Western Railway. This did not amuse his publishers, but such was his ability they ensured that the best process workers were used for his material. While producing drawings for *English Cathedrals* he sloped off to do work and left his wife to deal with the small talk and cucumber sandwiches at the tea parties of deans and bishops. On one occasion while sketching in Durham Cathedral he was locked in by mistake, so heaved on the bell ropes and brought the whole City running. The ensuing pandemonium caused him much satisfaction and amusement (100x110).

A soke was a piece of land which in medieval times lay outside the jurisdiction of the main authority of the area, the largest in England being that of Peterborough. In Winchester the Bishop controlled an area on the south-east of the City as his soke and in which William of Wykeham was careful to site his new College. The one arched stone bridge near the old demolished Eastgate, now only recalled by Eastgate Street, was also known as Soke Bridge with a mill close by it. This latter became a youth hostel, and immediately after the Second World War with fairly primitive washing facilities, had prohibitory notices forbidding the naked or half-naked to be carried out into the river. Whether this was to prevent ablutionists being precipitated over the nearby weirs, or merely that the good citizens of Winchester were more than usually susceptible to outrage at the sight of nakedness, was never made clear. At the top left a sketch by Charles G. Harper from the Reverend A.G. L'Estrange's *Royal Winchester* of 1889 (80x90). At the top right a drawing by Herbert Railton from *Our English Minsters* of 1893 edited by Frederic William Farrar (85x70). Below a watercolour by Wilfrid Williams Ball from the Reverend Telford Varley's *Hampshire* of 1909 (110x140). Bottom an undated but Edwardian drawing by Alexander Murray from the *Pilgrims' Way From Winchester to Canterbury* by Julia Cartwright (100 x 140).

HOOD · IN
SOVTHGATE · STREET

IN · THE
CLOSE.

IN PARCIMENT ST

A series of beautifully detailed drawings of eighteenth century doorways in various parts of the City. The artist is L.G. Detmar and the drawings are dated 1902. They are included in Volume 7 of The Third Series of the *Architectural Association's Sketchbooks* (whole page 380x280).

Two very similar views of the High Street with the Old Guildhall clock prominent on its bracket and the Butter Cross behind. The Old Guildhall of 1713 is now used for commercial purposes and has a statue of Queen Anne prominently placed in a centre niche. At the top an anonymous view published by T. Prouten of Winchester and engraved by Newman and Barclay (85x140). Below an engraving from Volume 3 of Robert Mudie's *Hampshire* of 1838. The artist is George Sidney Shepherd and the engravers are J. Shury and Son (105x150).

Three views of the Old Guildhall. Only the top storey was ever used for municipal purposes as the ground floor was in the hands of St John's Hospital. At the top a sketch by Charles G. Harper from the Reverend A.G. L'Estrange's *Royal Winchester* of 1889 (110x87). Below left a drawing by Percy Robertson from the Art Journal of 1890 (170x130). Below right a sketch by Jenny Wylie dated 1909 from Volume 5 of the *Victoria County History of Hampshire* of 1912 (115x95).

The New Guildhall built in 1873 by the architects Jeffrey and Skiller with a rear extension of 1893 by J.B. Colson. As often happens in municipal affairs, there was need for a supplementary estimate with heated discussion and harsh words before everything was finally agreed. The drawing is by Charles G. Harper and comes from *Royal Winchester* of 1889 by the Reverend A.G. L'Estrange (110x38).

The opening ceremony of the New Guildhall, which was performed by the Lord Chancellor, the Earl of Selborne, who stands foursquare in the middle of the balcony with the Bishop of Winchester and the local M.P. John Bonham Carter in close attendance. They are surrounded by a sea of top hats and obviously very important persons. However, in the bottom middle of the picture there is one sole person who has the temerity to sport a bowler hat. Perhaps he was the caretaker who had slid in among the V.I.P.s. This anonymous wood engraving comes from the *Illustrated London New*s of 24 May 1873 (160x240).

This seems to be an intelligent anticipation of the High Street pedestrianisation, which was to take place a century later. An anonymous wood engraving from the *Illustrated London News* of July 9 1887 showing a great beanfeast outside the New Guildhall to celebrate Queen Victoria's Golden Jubilee, which repays careful scrutiny for its fascinating detail. The dispensing of conscience salving Victorian charity to the deserving (and no doubt undeserving) poor seems equally divided between the ale and roast beef of Old (pre-B.S.E.) England (165x235).

A slap-up dinner in the former Corn Exchange in honour of the local M.P. John Bonham Carter and George Shaw Lefevre, the nephew of Lord Eversley. The assembled throng of four hundred guests settled down to demolish a cold collation and consume quantities of wine supplied 'in good style' by the appropriately name Mr Crate of the Market Inn. The building has a portico strongly reminiscent of Inigo Jones' St Paul, Covent Garden, and was opened in 1838. The architect is Owen Browne Carter and the building has now been converted into the City's public library. It would therefore be a pleasing conceit to think of the puzzled ghosts of ruddy-cheeked farmers trying to find their places for dinner amid the bookshelves. The sketch for this engraving from the *Illustrated London News* of 3 September 1859 'was supplied by Mr R. Baigent Junior of Winchester' (175x235).

At this long remove of a century and a half, it is difficult to appreciate the excitement caused by the 1848 revolutions in Europe, but in the same way that Garibaldi came to symbolize the Italian aspiration for a national identity, so did Kossuth's bid for Hungarian freedom catch the public imagination. He was welcomed as a hero in Britain and when the Austrian General Haynau, known as the Butcher of Hungary, was visiting Barclay Perkins Brewery in Southwark, he was chased off the premises by irate workers and suffered the indignity of having to take refuge in a dustbin. Kossuth landed in Southampton and was taken under the wing of the then Mayor of Southampton, Richard Andrews. He was received in both Southampton and Winchester with great enthusiasm, as the anonymous wood engravings from the *Illustrated London News* of 1 November 1851 on this and the following page make clear. Above the procession making its way with difficulty through an immense crowd near St Cross (110x230). Below left an almost equally large crowd listening to speeches near the City Mill (100x150). Below right ornate chinoiserie cottage of the Mayor of Southampton in Winchester where Kossuth was received (110x160).

Kossuth giving a speech in the Mayor of Southampton's cottage (120x160).

The Mayor of Southampton, Richard Andrews, himself (95x75).

A banquet given for Kossuth in Southampton Town Hall. This appears to be an all-male affair with the ladies adding style to an otherwise staid occasion (150x230).

Two undated sketches by A.L. Collins of the vaulted ground storey of a house in St Thomas' Street, which seems as with many basements and lofts to have become a repository for a collection of old junk. Both views come from *Volume 5 of the Victoria County History of Hampshire* of 1912 (on the left 127x100, on the right 100x127).

A rather stiff and lifeless drawing of College Street as it was in 1838 by Francis Joseph Baigent. It is included in the Reverend H.C. Adams *Wykehamica – History of Winchester College and Commoners* of 1878 (130x80).

A drawing of Royal Oak Passage between the High Street and St George's Street dated 18 May 1889 by Charles G. Harper. It comes from the Reverend A.G. L'Estrange's *Royal Winchester*, also of 1889 (140x76).

Three views by Owen Browne Carter from his *Picturesque Memorials of Winchester* of 1830. At the top left St John's Street with part of St John's Church. The engraver is William Tombleson (130x120). At the top right Colebrook Street with the Cathedral tower in the background (135x110). Below left the High Street looking towards the eastern face of the Westgate (135x120). The engraver for both the latter is John Le Keux. Below right a drawing of 1873 by Charles G. Harper from *Royal Winchester* of 1889 by the Reverend A.G. L'Estrange. This row of shops known variously as Penthouse, Pentice or Pentisse brings a touch of the rows of Chester or the arcades of Bologna and the North Italian towns to the City (105x90).

The brooks or open streams that once ran through the centre of the City that are now like the Fleet River cribbed, cabined and confined. On the left while still flowing from John Britton's *Cathedral Antiquities* of 1817. The artist is William Henry Bartlett and the engraver Samuel Williams (80x115). Below already in a conduit from a sketch of Middle Brook by Charles G. Harper dated June 1889 from the Reverend A.G. L'Estrange's *Royal Winchester* also of 1889 (95x140). Both views show the Cathedral tower over trees in the background.

Middle Brook.

The plan that never was. A lithograph by Day & Son of a proposed new layout of the High Street in 1848 by the architect Owen Browne Carter. From the Butter Cross the High Street would have run past a rebuilt St Lawrence Church to a new north-east entrance to the Cathedral Close, which was obviously modelled closely on the outer and middle gateways of Winchester College (290x415).

This page illustrates the English passion, so beloved of estate agents, of exposing olde oake beames, something our ancestors would have considered a form of nakedness by displaying the skeleton of a building. It is often also wise to enquire if exposed beams date from the 1530's or the 1930's. However, these premises in Cheesehill/Chesil Street are the genuine article and date from about the mid fifteenth century. They were formerly the Rectory of the Church of St Peter Chesil, which has now been converted into a theatre. At the top and centre two drawings by George Herbert Kitchen of 1892 showing before and after restoration from the *Proceedings of the Hampshire Field Club and Archaeological Society* of the same year (62x94 and 110x170). Below a sketch by Jenny Wylie dated 1908 in Volume 5 of the *Victoria County History of Hampshire* of 1912 (90x125).

The County Hospital in Parchment Street was opened at Michaelmas 1759 and replaced an earlier building in Colebrook Street, which was considered too small. By 1864 it too was deemed inadequate and in 1868 the premises designed by William Butterfield were completed on the present Romsey Road site. Since that date there have naturally been numerous additions to keep up with modern medical requirements. The Parchment Street building was initially a disaster area, as it was dogged by inadequate funds and the governing body's insistence on starting the process by buying a quarter of a million bricks to go it alone. This shambolic state of affairs was only relieved by the appointment of John Wood Junior, the son of the famous architect of Bath of the same name. He gradually sorted out the chaos and organised the building's completion, by which time it was being described as 'a magnificent edifice'. Wood's comments on that particular phrase might well have been interesting. The artist of this view is W. Cave and the engraver James Taylor. It was included in Thomas Warton's *History and Antiquities of Winchester* of 1773 and re-used without acknowledgement in the 1795 edition of the *Winchester Guide* (65x130).

A view of the almshouses of St John's Hospital South. The architect is William Garbett, but on his death in 1834, the trustees appointed his pupil Owen Browne Carter to complete the work. The lithograph is by Louis Haghe after one of Carter's own drawings (210x285).

The perpendicular gateway of Hyde Abbey off King Alfred Place is all that remains of one of the greatest Benedictine nunneries of England, which was originally founded more than a thousand years ago. This sketch by Jenny Wylie dated 1908 comes from Volume 5 of the *Victoria County History of Hampshire*, of 1912 (65x75).

The buildings of Hyde Abbey still remaining in the eighteenth century when they were being used for farm purposes. Both engravings come from Francis Grose's *Antiquities*. The first edition was from 1773 to 1776 with supplements in 1777 and 1787, but it was also issued in parts as well as being bound up in book form. The artist for most of the watercolours used in the engravings is Grose himself, but there is no specific attribution for either of these two views. The engraver of the centre view is the enigmatic 'D.L.' and it is dated 1 May 1783, while the engraver of the view below is Thomas Bonnor with the date of 10 January 1784. A large number of Grose's original watercolours are in the collections of the Society of Antiquaries (both 110x155).

At the top an engraving of the Great Hall of Winchester Castle by James Newton dated 8 January 1787 from Francis Grose's *Antiquities* (115x155).

Below another view of the Great Hall by one of the Shepherd family of topographical artists without any initials to enable a precise identification. There are certainly a large number of what appear to be visitors standing around, and what exactly is the gentleman in some kind of uniform on the left doing with that placard? Is he proclaiming that the end of the world is nigh or advertising some sort of product? The engravers are J. Shury and Son and the view comes from Volume 3 of Robert Mudie's *Hampshire* of 1838 (105x150).

A sketch of the Great Hall by Charles G. Harper from the Reverend A.G. L'Estrange's *Royal Winchester* of 1889 (85x140).

Elevations of an exterior and interior bay of the Great Hall. Both are drawn by Owen Browne Carter and engraved by Philip Henry Delamotte and John Smith Heaviside. They come from the *Proceedings* of the Archaeological Institute's visit to Winchester of 1845 (Exterior 82x64, Interior 55x93).

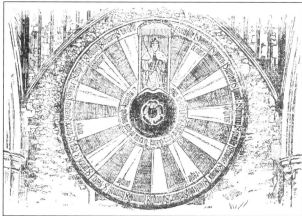

The round table. This venerable piece of timber with a tudor rose at the centre was first mentioned in the fifteenth century, but was not new then. It would be interesting to know what running repairs have had to be done over the intervening centuries and what was its original function. The anonymous drawing on the left is from Charles Oman's *Castles* of 1926 (58x93). The engraving on the right is No. 1671 by Rock and Company dated 20 July 1851 (70x70).

An east view of the Palace designed for Charles II by Sir Christopher Wren, which was completed in 1685 (see also page 16). This view is drawn and engraved by the brothers Samuel and Nathaniel Buck and dated 1733. The brothers' prodigious output of engravings of buildings and town panoramas from 1720 onwards was re-issued in two volumes in 1774 by Robert Sayer as Bucks' *Antiquities*. This view is one of more than four hundred in Volume 1 while Volume 2 contains almost one hundred town panoramas (see also page 9) (145x350).

Another east view, this time 'taken on the spot by an officer'. The engraver is D.S. Peak and it appears in Volume 7 of the *Wren Society* publications of 1930 (75x190).

A further view drawn by James Cave after Sir Christopher Wren and engraved by J. Pass. It is also from Volume 7 of the *Wren Society* publications of 1930 (200x340).

A crude engraving entitled 'A View of the Ruins of the King's Palace' from Thomas Warton's *History and Antiquities of Winchester* of 1773. The artist is W. Cave and the engravers Dent and Innes. The two minute figures in the foreground are totally out of proportion with the rest of the drawing (75x160).

The Palace when in use as a barracks with the cow on the right rather detracting from the martial air of the soldiery. The drawing is by George Shepherd and the engravers are J. Shury and Son. It comes from Volume 3 of Robert Mudie's *Hampshire* of 1838 (100x150).

An anonymous and undated engraving published by T. Prouten of Winchester, also showing the Palace being used as a barracks. A soldier on the left has taken off his bearskin and sits on his drum, while the person lounging on the coping of what is presumably a well head, seems to be an officer with a swagger stick keeping an eye on the rather desultory drilling going on to his right (65x150).

The Stanmore Estate due west of Winchester College. Two plans of designs for the City Council by William Curtis Green from the *Builder* of November 23 1923. The Estate has since had seventy five years to mature into a very pleasant appearance. Curtis Green was also a brilliant draughtsman and his exquisite and detailed drawings of buildings in England and on the Continent are matched by an equally attractive, but freer watercolour style, placing buildings in a landscape. He was a self-confessed traditionalist in architectural matters and his firm William Curtis Son and Lloyd is responsible for Barclays Bank of 1957-1959 at the Corner of Jewry Street (each 120x170).

THE CATHEDRAL

The Normans were Vikings in origin and when William landed in England and won the battle of Hastings, he brought with him a band of tough, dedicated men full of restless energy. Many Normans in the medieval period were also to fan out into southern Europe and the Near East, both as soldiers of fortune and conquerors of substantial kingdoms. Those that had come to England set about stamping their authority on this new realm with vast building projects. In addition to castles and fortifications, monastic houses were founded and cathedrals constructed. Indeed, in the century after 1080 most of the cathedrals and many of the great abbeys churches were built or rebuilt.

There is still a great deal of confusion about who did what in the medieval construction industry. By and large bishops and abbots were what we now recognise as clients for ecclesiastical projects and having outlined a brief either fairly vaguely or in great detail, would leave matters for a master mason to carry forward. The latter really combined the skills of an architect, building and contractor and would employ a workforce to bring matters to completion.

Sometimes in monastic foundations monks would do some of the hard graft of fetching and carrying, but in reality the great British workman was already alive, well and leaning on his spade, and it was from the laity that he would have been overwhelmingly recruited. Perhaps the most outstanding master mason to work on the Cathedral was William of Wynford in the Wykeham episcopate (1366-1404). He had been at Windsor Castle and Wells Cathedral during Wykeham's earlier appointments and in addition to the Cathedral worked at Winchester College and New College, Oxford. He was clearly a man of great skill and at the top of his chosen profession.

Walkelin was the first Norman Bishop of Winchester (1070-1097) and a relative of the Conqueror. His new cathedral had to take into account the proximity of the Saxon Minster during the construction period and the immense length of the nave may be because the Norman West front was intended to approximate in position to that of the Minster, which was demolished on completion of the new works. It could also have been an attempt to emulate the size of Constantine's St Peter's church in Rome or because it was second only to Westminster in royal associations. On the other hand it might have been simply an intention to overawe with an element of keeping up with the Jones's in the shape of what other bishops were building. Probably at the end of the day it was a mixture of all these considerations and in any event they were nearer earthly ambition than heavenly adoration.

Building work started in 1079 and was completed by 1093, an astonishing performance by any standards for so large a project. The massive solidity of construction was a statement of enormous self confidence by a man who was not only a bishop, but also a force to be reckoned with in the running of the whole country. God was very obviously now seen to be on the side of the victorious Normans instead of the defeated Saxons. For possible stylistic sources one must look in Normandy to the church of St Etienne at Caen, the Abbey of Jumieges and especially Rouen Cathedral, while in England St Augustine's Abbey in Canterbury seems a likely candidate.

The fabric of any great cathedral is a palimpsest on which successive generations have left their mark. Styles change, stone decays, sudden collapses occur and often buttresses are needed to shore up foundations. As time moved on the austere power of Walkelin's romanesque was altered by Edington (1345-1366) and then Wykeham (1366-1404) and this is nowhere more obvious than in the nave. The visitor approaching the Cathedral at its west end sees a facade where the porches and side windows date from the Edington period, whereas the great west window, the biggest in the building, must be dated to Wykeham's episcopate. Inside the change from Edington to Wykeham occurs after the first aisle window on the south side and the second on the north. Beyond these changes – the full flower of the perpendicular becomes apparent.

However, it is in the north and south transepts that Walkelin's romanesque can still be seen clearly, although overlaid with later decorated and perpendicular work. Two important areas of the building which were modified before the Edington period are the Retrochoir and Lady Chapel. These changes mainly took place in the episcopate of de Lucy (1189-1204), although he did not live to see them completed and again they have been further re-fashioned.

Restoration became imperative in the nineteenth century and there two periods of this activity from 1812 to 1828 and again from 1874 to 1891. The former was overseen by William Garbett and the latter by John Colson. In the early twentieth century there was an even more dangerous situation to cope with, as the very foundations of the building were waterlogged and had to be underpinned by the expedient of sending down a diver, William Walker, who over a six year period inserted 25,000 bags of concrete, 115,000 concrete blocks and 900,000 bricks into this yawning and murky chasm. In addition, the consulting engineer Francis Fox, and the architect Thomas (later Sir Thomas) Jackson, added the buttresses on the south side to strengthen the structure of the building further.

The magnificence and majesty of the fabric of the Cathedral is matched by the sumptuousness of the interior. The font with its Tournai marble, the chantries of Waynflete, Wykeham, Beanfort and Fox and the many other memorials and tombs, the beautiful choir stalls dating from 1308, the splendid range of medieval encaustic tiles in the Retrochoir and the choir screen and great screen all combine to provide a rich feast for the eye and a deep sense of history stretching back over nine hundred years.

A north view of the Cathedral. It appeared originally in Sir William Dugdale's *Monasticon Anglicanum* published between 1655 and 1673. The artist is Richard Newcourt and the engraver Daniel King who is thought to have died in 1664. The latter published a selection of the engravings from the *Monasticon* in 1656 under the title *Cathedrall and Conventuall Churches of England and Wales*. King's etchings are fairly crude, but nevertheless give an early record of architectural features, which were later modified. Dugdale had a low opinion of King and described him as 'an ignorant silly fellow … an arrant knave'. This engraving had a long life and was copied with trifling alterations by M.V. de Gucht for Samuel Gale's *History and Antiquities of the Cathedral Church of the Holy Trinity in Winton* in 1715 (155x280).

An engraving entitled 'North East View of Winchester Cathedral', which appears in John Milner's *History of Winchester* (1798-1801). The artist is James Cave and the engraver J. Pass. This version is dated 1 March 1809 and comes from the second edition of Milner's work (275x480).

John Britton (1771-1857) was an indefatigable worker and publisher of a number of topographical works, who kept meticulous records. A three month tour of the West Country cost him £11 16s 9d and viewing Blenheim Palace alone set him back the then enormous sum of 2s 6d. He was an incredible walker and had covered three and a half thousand miles by the end of only the fifth volume of the *Beauties of England and Wales* and it is perhaps therefore no wonder that he lived to a ripe old age. It is also not surprising that a man with this background should demand the highest standards for his publications and employed the best process workers of his day. This is the first of a number of copper engravings from Britton's *Cathedral Antiquities* and is a view of the north transept of the Cathedral dated 1 March 1817. The artist is Edward Blore and the engraver John Le Keux. Britton could hardly have endeared himself to his contemporaries, as when writing about the chantries of several of the Bishops of Winchester, which were illustrated in the Society of Antiquities publication *Vetusta Monumenta* and were produced by the Society's engraver James Basire from drawings by Jacob Schnebbelie, he says 'Had these plates been accurately drawn and engraved, they would have proved highly interesting and valuable; but the slovenly style in which they were executed, seems rather to tantalize than to gratify our curiosity' (210x150).

A view of the north transept of the Cathedral from Volume 1 of B. Winkles' *Cathedral Churches of England and Wales* of 1836-1842 with a text by Thomas Moule, whose fame rests much more on his excellent cartographic work. The view is drawn by Hablot Browne from a sketch by Robert Garland and the engraver is W.E. Albutt. This is one of Hablot Browne's earliest works and he went on to become one of the best known of the illustrators of Charles Dickens novels with the nickname 'Phiz' (112x145).

No 1096 of Rock and Co.'s engravings entitled 'N.E. View of Winchester Cathedral'. It is anonymous and undated (65x90).

A wood engraving entitled 'Winchester Cathedral – A General View from the North West'. It comes from Richard John King's *Handbook to the Cathedrals of England* published by John Murray in 1861. The artist and engraver is Orlando Jewitt (95x145).

A north east view of the Cathedral from Volume 4 of James Sargant Storer's *History and Antiquities of the Cathedral Churches of Great Britain* of 1819. This engraving was produced by Storer himself from a drawing by his son Henry Sargant Storer. It is dated 1 September 1813 (78x115).

Rock & Co.'s engraving No. 922 entitled 'Winchester Cathedral – View of the North Transept'. It is anonymous and undated (80x65).

An engraving entitled 'View of the North Side of the Choir Etc from the North East' from John Britton's *Cathedral Antiquities* which is dated 2 December 1816. The artist is Edward Blore and the engraver John Le Keux (158x212).

A south east view of the Cathedral from the ruins of Wolvesey from Volume 4 of James Sargant Storer's *History and Antiquities of the Cathedral Churches of Great Britain* dated 1 September 1813. The engraver is Storer himself and the artist his son Henry (78x115).

An engraving somewhat quaintly entitled 'Winchester Old Minster, Now the Cathedral, Hampshire' from Volume 5 of Francis Grose's *Antiquities of England and Wales*. The artist is Samuel Hooper and the engraver James Newton. The engraving is dated 1 January 1787 (110x160).

An undated engraving entitled 'South View of Winchester Cathedral' from Volume 4 of James Sargant Storer's *History and Antiquities of the Cathedral Churches of Great Britain* of 1819. The engraving is by Storer himself from a drawing by his son Henry. A pleasant domestic touch is given by the man carrying a ladder on the left and another digging on the right (78x115).

A sketch by Herbert Marshall entitled the 'Cathedral from the South East' from *Winchester College 1393 to 1893* by Old Wykehamists (155x200).

A sketch by Joseph Pennell dated 1885 entitled also the 'Cathedral from the South East'. It is from Mrs Schuyler Van Rensselaer's *English Cathedrals* of 1887 and shows a tête à tête on the lawn at the back of the Bishop's Palace. On the right is a net in position for tennis (83x130).

An almost identical view as the one above. A sketch by Herbert Railton from F.W. Farrer's *Our English Minsters* of 1893. The boy seems to be offering the girl some kind of posy (85x152).

The east end of the Cathedral. An engraving from John Britton's *Cathedral Antiquities* drawn by Edward Blore and engraved by R. Sands. It is dated 1 January 1818 and the sheep add a pleasing rural touch (209x158).

A similar but undated view to that on the previous page from Volume 1 of B. Winkles'
Cathedral Churches of England and Wales of 1836-1842. The artist is Robert Garland and
the engraver Winkles himself. The figure in the foreground certainly seems to be rather curiously dressed (111x145).

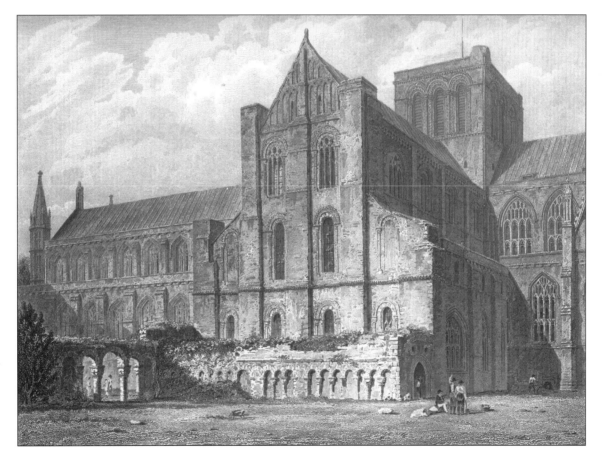

An engraving dated 1 August 1817 from John Britton's *Cathedral Antiquities* entitled South Transept with Ruins of the
Chapter House. The artist is Edward Blore and the engraver R. Sands and the view exhibits a good deal of activity. At the
extreme right a workman is pushing a wheelbarrow, while in the right foreground a workman in true British tradition is
leaning on his spade and chatting with friends. Just to the left of this little group somebody inspects the pointed arch. The
workman has left his barrow on the left for somebody to trip over and on the extreme left under the arcade visitors admire
the Cathedral (160x210).

The nave and west end of the Cathedral, a line drawing by the prolific artist T. Raffles Davison, who produced some ten thousand 'rambling sketches' for the *British Architect* and other publications. This view is from the *Art Journal* of 1888 (128x167).

A view drawn and etched by John Chessel Buckler from his *Views of Cathedral Churches of England and Wales* of 1822 and entitled 'Winchester Cathedral N.W'. The Buckler family John, who was John Chessel's father and Charles Alban, John Chessel's son, produced vast quantities of topographical work and some twelve thousand drawings alone by the three were left by Charles Alban to the British Library Department of Manuscripts. This etching is dated 2 November 1817 (180x255).

An engraving entitled 'North West View of the Cathedral' from Volume 2 of John Milner's *History of Winchester* of 1809. The artist is John Carter and the engraver James Basire (105x130).

Another north west view which is engraving No. 1176 by Rock & Co. It shows visitors admiring the Cathedral and a flock of sheep in the background. The engraving is anonymous and undated (60x90).

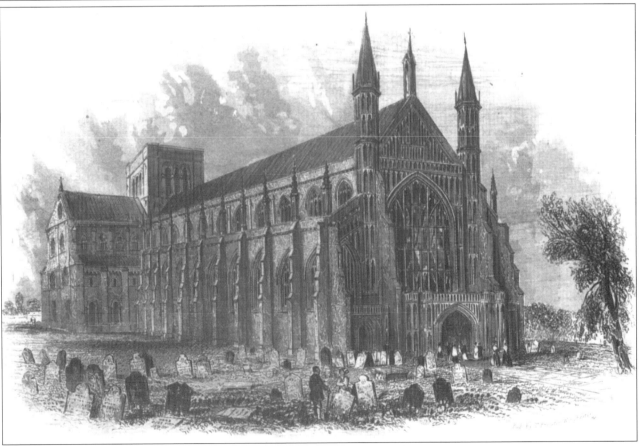

A similar view to those above with a woman talking to the sexton in the foreground. The anonymous and undated engraving is a publication by T. Prouten of Winchester (105x60).

The west front of the Cathedral, an engraving by B. Winkles from a drawing by Hablot Browne in Volume 1 of Winkles' own *Cathedral Churches of England and Wales* of 1836 to 1842 (140x110).

A view entitled the 'Nave and Transept from the North West' by Joseph Pennell from Mrs Schuyler Van Rensselaer's *English Cathedrals* of 1887. The wood engraving is by H.E. Sylvester (89x132).

This powerful engraving by J. Shury is based on a drawing by G.H. Shepherd and included in Volume 3 of Robert Mudie's *Hampshire* of 1838. Is the artist in fact George Sidney Shepherd as there appears to be no G.H. Shepherd among the numerous progeny of the famous Shepherd family of topographical artists? Storm clouds are gathering and a deluge cannot be far away as birds circle the tower (105x50).

The long walk up to the west door of the Cathedral seen as summer and winter views by Joseph Pennell from Mrs Schuyler Van Rensselaer's *English Cathedrals* of 1887. The summer view is a wood engraving by C.J. Waddell (110x75) and the winter view a straightforward line drawing based on a photograph (88x115). The reliance that some nineteenth century artists placed on photography is an intriguing subject in its own right, but certainly in this instance it has helped Pennell to produce a striking drawing.

The west front of the Cathedral shown in an undated engraving by James Sargant Storer from Volume 4 of his work the *History and Antiquities of the Cathedral Churches of Great Britain* of 1819. It is based on a drawing by his son Henry (115x178).

The west front of the Cathedral drawn by Joseph Pennell and reproduced as a wood engraving by K.C. Atwood for Mrs Schuyler Van Renssaelare's *English Cathedrals* of 1887 (87x64).

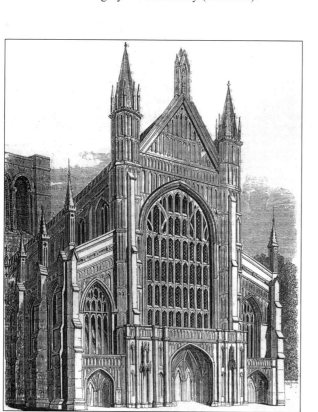

Old England is a vast jackdaw collection of mostly anonymous small wood engravings edited by Charles Knight. It first appeared in 1845 and is based on the popular magazines of the period, designed to promote national pride in British institutions and achievements. This competent anonymous engraving is No. 671 (155x135).

William Howitt's *Visits to Remarkable Places* first appeared in 1840 and is a series of descriptions of locations all over the British Isles. This wood engraved view of the west front of the Cathedral is from the second edition of 1888 and the artist is Samuel Williams (85x75).

The west front of the Cathedral from John Britton's *Cathedral Antiquities*. It is engraved by John Le Keux from a drawing by Edward Blore and dated 1 May 1817 (230x170).

A finely detailed engraving of a section and plan of the west front of the Cathedral, also from John Britton's *Cathedral Antiquities*. The artist is Edward Blore and the engraver Edmund Turrell with a date of 2 December 1816 (230x150).

A south east view of the Cathedral drawn and etched by John Chessel Buckler for his Views of the *Cathedral Churches of England and Wales* of 1822. It is very similar to a larger version by his father John Buckler of September 1808. This view is dated 2 Nov 1817 (180x255).

An anonymous engraved view of the Cathedral very similar to that above. The engraving firm is Newman and Barclay of London and the publisher T. Prouten of Winchester (105x140).

A drawing by Alfred Rimmer which comes from his book *Ancient Streets and Homesteads of England* of 1877 (70x95).

Two engraved views of the Cathedral. Above a south-west view and below a north-west view. The raising of the ladder in the latter is obviously a delicate and precision operation. Both are from Volume 4 of James Sargant Storer's *History and Antiquities of the Cathedral Churches of Great Britain* of 1819. The engraver is Storer himself and the artist his son Henry (both 78x115).

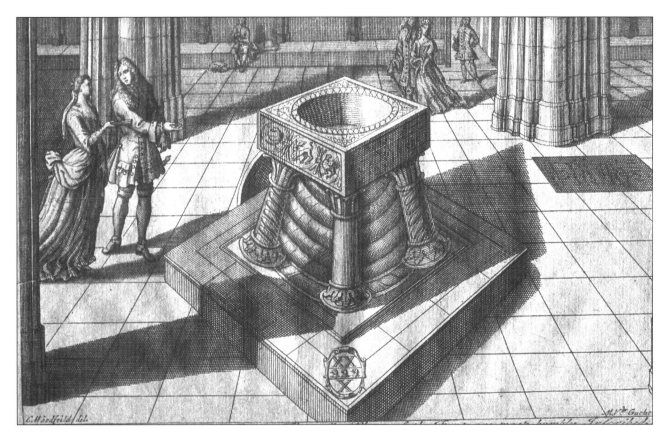

A curious view from above of the medieval font in the north aisle of the nave. It comes from Samuel Gale's *History and Antiquities of the Cathedral Church of the Holy Trinity in Winton* of 1715. The artist is Charles Woodfeild (sic) and the engraver M.V. de Gucht. The font dates from the 1150s or 1160s and reflects Bishop Henry de Blois' considerable interest in sculpture. It is of black marble and was imported from Tournai and is the finest of a group of nine or ten in England. Three of the others are also in Hampshire: at All Saints', East Meon, St Mary Bourne and St Michael's Southampton, all within a 15 mile radius of Winchester itself (100x110).

Detailed drawings of the font from John Carter's *Ancient Architecture of England* of 1795-1814. Two sides depict stories of St Nicholas, the third three roundels with birds and the fourth a salamander flanked by two birds. The view from above shows two spandrels with leaf designs and two with birds drinking from a vase. Font (L) 80x90 Plan (M) 44x86 Bowl from above (N) 90x90 North Front (P) 30x87 South and West Fronts (Q and R) 62x172. The drawings are of 1789, but the publication date is June 1 1799. Carter was appointed draughtsman to the Society of Antiquaries in 1795 and campaigned for many years in the *Gentleman's Magazine* against the destruction and insensitive restoration of ancient buildings.

Engravings depicting the south and west fronts of the font. They are from John Britton's *Cathedral Antiquities* and are dated 1 November 1816. The artist is Edward Blore and the engraver John Le Keux (Above 102x147, Below 110x147).

WEST SIDE.

EAST AND NORTH SIDES

SOUTH SIDE.

The font from Reginald John King's *Handbook to the Cathedrals of England.* The date is 1861 and the artist and engraver Orlando Jewitt (the two panels 31x82, the font 80x87).

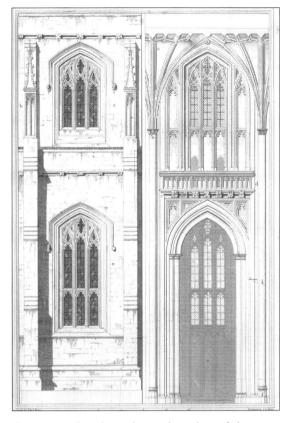

Robert Willis was the Professor of Natural Experimental Philosophy at Cambridge (1832-1875) and among a wide variety of interests a noted archaeologist and architectural historian. For the Archaeological Institute's visit to Winchester in 1845 he produced a paper on the Cathedral's construction, which was published separately in the following year. In this paper he included a diagram of the transformation of the nave profiles from romanesque to the perpendicular so familiar today. Although Willis did not include parallels with other European ecclesiastical architecture and there is much discussion still about what exactly should be attributed to the episcopate of Edington (1346-1366) compared with that of Wykeham (1367-1404), his work has largely stood the test of time and was widely copied in later publications on the Cathedral. This version is from Reginald John King's Handbook to the *Cathedrals of England* of 1861 (140x100).

One external and one internal section of the nave after its transformation into perpendicular. From John Britton's *Cathedral Antiquities*, the artist being Edward Blore and engraver John Le Keux. The date is 1 February 1815 (externally 230x75, internally 220x157).

Professor Willis lecturing at the Archaeological Institute's 1845 meeting in Winchester at the St John's Hall. A close examination of the scene reveals a great deal of chit-chat going on at what many people regarded as a merely social occasion. The lady at the front on the left appears to have been overcome by boredom and is pleading to be taken away by her escort. Willis must have found lecturing in these circumstances tedious in the extreme. An anonymous wood engraving from the *Illustrated London News* of 20 September 1845 (140x150).

Edmund Sharpe (1809-1877) was an architect who trained as a pupil of Thomas Rickman. He practised at Lancaster from 1836 to 1851 and then moved over to engineering during the period of the great railway expansion in England. He published a number of architectural works and these finely detailed engravings of two external and two internal bays of the Cathedral come from his *Seven Periods of Architecture* of 1851 (external 175x111, internal 175x105).

A view in the nave showing the font and William of Wykeham's Chantry. It is from Volume 1 of B. Winkles' *Cathedral Churches of England and Wales* of 1836-1842 with a text by Thomas Moule. The artist is Hablot Browne and the engraver Winkles himself (148x100).

A view across the nave showing the perpendicular features clearly. It is from John Britton's *Cathedral Antiquities* and the date is 1 October 1816. The artist is Edward Blore and the engraver William Radclyffe (225x160).

Another view across the nave dated September 1892, which in this instance looks south-west. It is by A. Needham Wilson and comes from the *Builder* of 1 October 1892 (285x180).

A glimpse through the west door looking eastwards down the nave. It comes from Volume 4 of James Sargant Storer's *History and Antiquities of the Cathedral Churches of Great Britain* and is dated 1 September 1813. The artist and engraver are Storer himself (78x117).

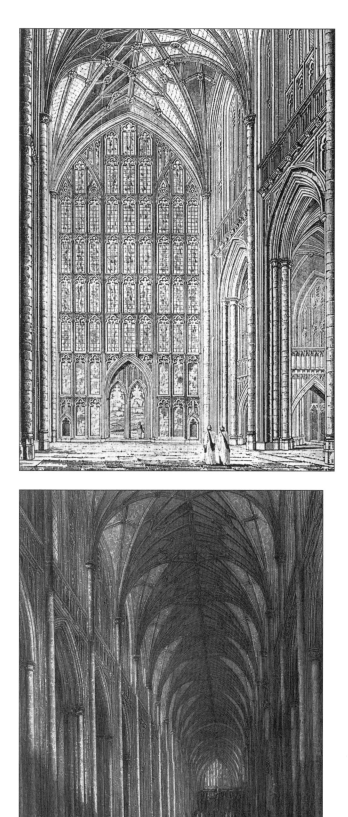

The great west window with its height and majesty emphasised by the two clerics in conversation on the right and the diminutive figure in the doorway pausing with hat in hand before entering. An engraving which appeared both in John Britton's *Chronological History of English Architecture* and also his *History of English Architecture*. The artist is Edward Blore and the engraver John Le Keux with a date of 1 May 1821 (200x148).

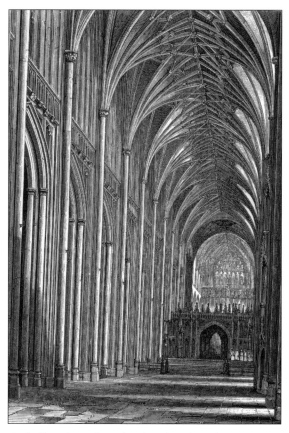

Two similar views. On the left from Volume 1 of B. Winkles' *Cathedral Churches of England and Wales* of 1836-1842. The artist is Hablot Browne and the engraver Winkles himself (140x110). On the right from Reginald John King's *Handbook to the Cathedrals of England* of 1861 with the artist and engraver being Orlando Jewitt (135x95). Both feature the screen by William Garbett of 1820, which replaced that of Inigo Jones.

A drawing by R.M.D. Lucas from the *Building News* of 14 October 1892, which shows clearly the intricate wooden vaulting under the tower and the flat ceilings put in the transepts in the 1820s (275x175).

Details of arches and parts of the tower from John Britton's *Cathedral Antiquities* with a date of 1 March 1817. The artist is Edward Blore and the engraver G. Hollis (162x210).

A finely detailed cut-away drawing looking straight into the Cathedral from the west end from John Britton's *Cathedral Antiquities*. It shows the Inigo Jones' choir screen and the great screen with the east window. North is on the left and south on the right of the engraving with the tower prominent in the centre. The artist is Charles Ferdinand Porden and the engraver Henry Le Keux, the young brother of John Le Keux. The date is 1 September 1817 (150x220).

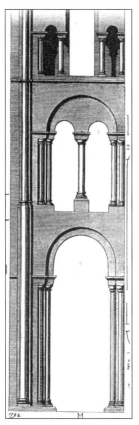

One division of a transept from John Carter's *Ancient Architecture of England* dated 1794 and published on 1 June 1797 (70x72).

A view of the north transept drawn and engraved by James Sargant Storer from Volume 4 of his *History and Antiquities of the Cathedral Churches of Great Britain*. It is dated 1 September 1813 (120x78).

One of Edward Blore's finely drawn views of the Cathedral. It shows the north transept looking north east and is from John Britton's *Cathedral Antiquities*. It is engraved by R. Sands and dated 1 March 1817. The woman in the background at the left clutches a baby and holds the hand of a small child. The boy sitting at the base of the pillar in the centre seems to have escaped from parental control and is doing his own thing (210x155).

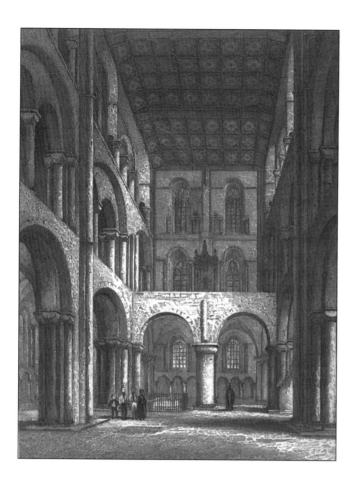

A view in the north transept engraved by W. Griffith from a drawing by Robert Garland in Volume 1 of B. Winkles' *Cathedral Churches of England and Wales* of 1836-1842. A family party on the left is discussing some point about the structure, but who is the rather mysterious and seemingly clerical figure in the background on the right? (145x112).

Another sketch of the north transept, being the work of Sir Thomas Graham Jackson from his *Byzantine and Romanesque Architecture* of 1913, the year in which he was made a baronet (151x112).

Prior Thomas Silkstede's chapel in the south transept as seen by Owen Browne Carter from his *Picturesque Memorials of Winchester* of 1830, Silkstede was Prior from 1498 to 1524 (175x130).

A view in the south transept by George Herbert Kitchen from the *Builder* of 1 October 1891 (285x180).

Detailing in Prior Thomas Silkstede's chapel in the south transept, which shows clearly his initials incorporated into the top of the screen. From a sketch by R.M.D. Lucas in the *Builder* of 15 July 1893 (156x185).

Two views in the choir looking towards the great screen and altar. That on the left is a wood engraving from the *Illustrated London News* of 15 April 1854 (325x235) and on the right a line drawing by Joseph Pennell of 1887 engraved by J.A. Naylor in Mrs Schuyler Van Rensselaer's *English Cathedrals* of the same date (175x114).

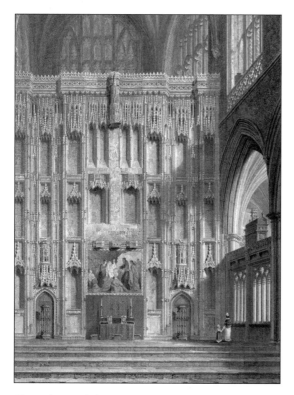

Two views of the great screen. That on the left is by Edward Blore and engraved by Henry Le Keux for John Britton's *Cathedral Antiquities*. It is dated 1 July 1817 (205x155). That on the right is drawn and engraved on wood by Orlando Jewitt for Reginald John King's *Handbook to the Cathedrals of England* of 1861 (118x85). All four illustrations on this page feature the great screen and Benjamin West's painting of the Raising of Lazarus which was placed in position in 1781 and John Wesley found 'far too glaring'. It was removed in 1899 after a long period of alteration and renovation to the screen and its statuary.

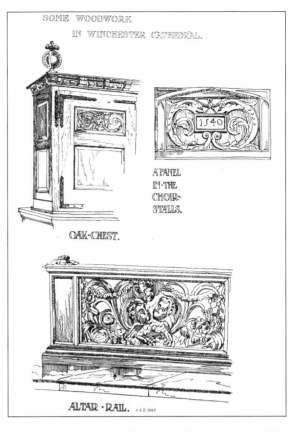

Looking westwards from the choir with detailing of the woodwork of the stalls, part of the tower and the whole length of the nave ceiling. In the foreground is the so-called Rufus tomb topped with Purbeck marble, now thought much more likely to be that of Henry de Bois. This simple monument either to a king or somebody with a close connection to royalty is in marked contrast to the elaborate chantries in the Cathedral, thought necessary by a number of diocesan bishops. The artist is Edward Blore and the engraver William Radclyffe. The view comes from John Britton's *Cathedral Antiquities* and is dated 1 January 1818 (205x160).

A panel in the choir stalls, an oak chest and part of the altar rail of 1640. This selection of details of woodwork in the Cathedral comes from Volume 7 of the third series of the *Architectural Association's Sketchbooks*. It is dated September 1901 and the artist is J. Harold Gibbons (panel 66x112, oak chest 115x75, altar rail 140x170).

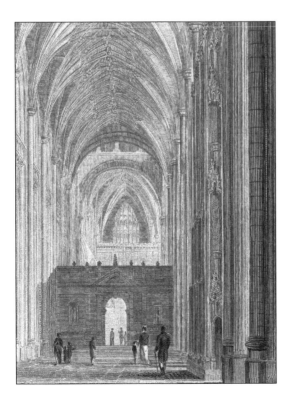

The choir screen by Inigo Jones of 1638, which featured bronze statues of James I and Charles I by Le Soeur. It survived until 1820 when it was replaced by William Garbett's gothic screen, itself replaced in turn by the present one in 1875 by Sir George Gilbert Scott. The drawing is from Britton's *Cathedral Antiqities*, 1 January 1818 (210x160), the engraving by H.C. Edwards after a drawing by Edward Blore.

Six sets of stained glass from the east window of the choir, drawn at slightly differing dates by Owen Browne Carter for his work *A Series of the Ancient Painted Glass of Winchester Cathedral* of 1845. At the top from the left St Paul, William of Wykeham and St Swithun, all of 1 March 1844. Below from the left Bishop Fox dated 1 June 1844, the prophet Jeremiah dated July 1 1844 and St. Andrew dated 1 October 1844 (all except Bishop Fox 384x80, Bishop Fox is 200x80).

At the top an engraving of part of the fourteenth century choir stalls from John Britton's *Cathedral Antiquities* dated 1 December 1816. The artist is Edward Blore and the engraver John Le Keux (200x160). In contrast at the bottom left another section of stalls drawn and engraved on wood by Orlando Jewitt. It comes from Reginald John King's *Handbook to the Cathedrals of England* of 1861 (110x75).

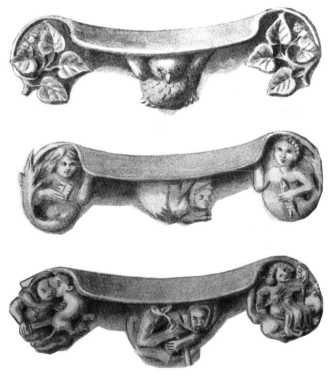

A section of the misericords under the seats on the north side of the choir stalls. At the top an owl with outspread wings with leaf decoration (40x130). In the centre a human head flanked by mermaids holding a comb and a fish (both 40x130). Below a fool bishop in a cap with long ears clasping a pastoral staff with his hands, accompanied on the left by a hooded man having his cheek bitten by a wolf or dog and on the right a woman in a hair net with a distaff and bodkin and a cat in the background (40x135).

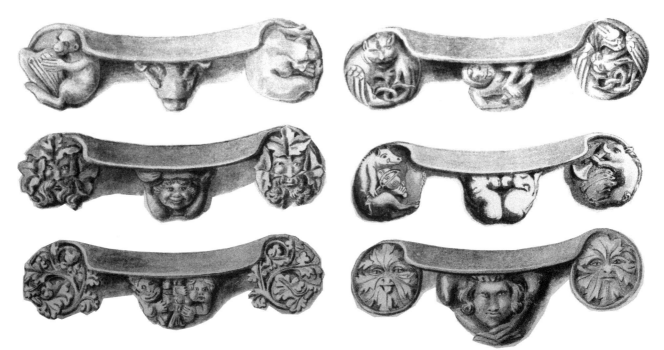

Above left and right more of the misericords on the north side of the choir stalls. At the top left a ram's head with curling horns with an ape playing a harp and a curled-up dog (35x135). Below a face and arms flanked by two foliated masks (35x130) and below that again two Davenport brothers (ie imposters who claimed spirits would untie their bound hands) with two sets of foliation (45x130). At the top right a fool or posture maker lying on his side and attempting to draw his sword with his right hand while the left holds the scabbard. His head lolls on one side and his tongue is stuck out. On either side a winged monster and two fighting dragons (35x135). Underneath two dogs with muzzles together, a boar playing a viol while another listens and a sow playing a pipe while feeding her litter (35x130). Finally a crouched man with hands round his knees and two foliated masks, one with a protruding tongue (45x130). Below left and right are misericords on the south side of the choir stalls. At the left top a masked figure or an ape with his arm round the neck of another ape in female dress flanked by a woman playing a double pipe and a viol (40x130). Below this a half figure of an upside down man with human heads or harpies in foliage (40x125). At the right top a woman seated flanked by boys in foliage (40x130). Below this a fox biting his near hind foot with two sets of leaves (40x125). At the bottom a harpy with large talons and two sets of leaves (40x135). All the misericords on this and the previous page are by Emma Phipson from her book *Choir Stalls and their Carving* of 1896. The photolithography is by Sprague and Company. Although many of these images would have been common in the outside world, it is intriguing to wonder how many could have come from inside the Cathedral itself. This seems hard to imagine in the antiseptic days of the late twentieth century, but it should be recorded that even in August 1998 an urban fox had to be removed from St Paul's Cathedral after sheltering for some time appropriately under the choir stalls, while trotting ahead of processing clergy and choir from time to time and causing mayhem by nibbling chocolate bars in the Cathedral bookshop. The smells it created were also medieval and caused great offence to twentieth century nostrils.

A view of three compartments on the north side of the lady chapel with wall paintings shown clearly on the right. The artist is Edward Blore and the engraver J. Roffe. It comes from John Britton's *Cathedral Antiquities* and is dated 1 May 1817 (150x220).

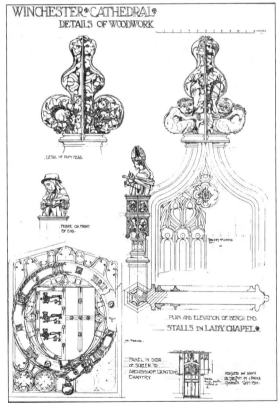

The wall paintings on the north and south sides of the lady chapel. This panel and those on the following page are scenes from the miracles of the Virgin. They come from John Carter's *Specimens of Ancient Sculpture and Paintings* and this panel is dated 1 April 1785 (265x335).

Details of the woodwork in the lady chapel and the adjoining Langton chantry. The artist is J. Harold Gibbons and the drawing dated September 1901 comes from Volume 7 of the third series of the *Architectural Association's Sketch Books* (380x280).

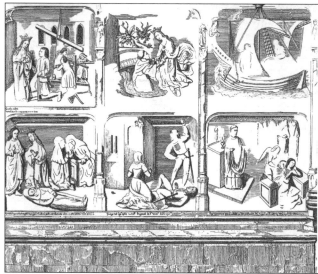

The panel at the top from the north side of the lady chapel is dated 1 November 1784 (270x385). The one at the centre from the south side is dated 1 November 1785 (255x310) and that below, also from the south side, 1 July 1785 (255x380). What the visitor sees today, however, are panels placed over the originals in the 1930s.

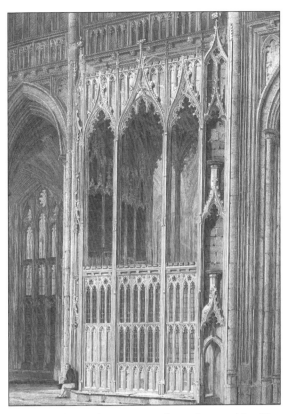

The Cathedral is greatly enriched by a number of splendid chantries to former bishops. At the top left the chantry of William of Wykeham, the founder of Winchester College and New College, Oxford. The artist is Richard Hamilton Essex and the engravers Henry Winkles and Joseph Skelton. The view comes from Skelton's *Pietas Oxoniensis* of 1828 and is dated more precisely as 1 May 1828. The engravings from this work were sold separately later and some bear dates after 1828 (270x190).

The Wykeham chantry seen from the outside. The artist is Edward Blore and the engraver William Radclyffe. The engraving is from John Britton's *Cathedral Antiquities* and is dated 1 June 1817 (210x155).

Wykeham's elaborate episcopal crozier. The artist and engraver is Orlando Jewitt and it was used in several works. This version is from Mackenzie E.C. Walcott's *William of Wykeham and His Colleges* of 1852 (crozier 150x20, detailed head of crozier 150x45).

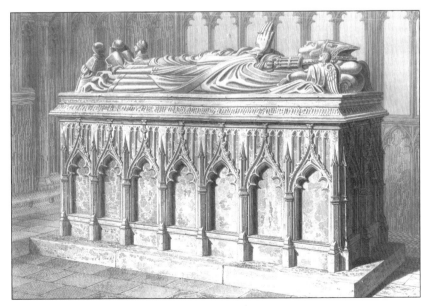

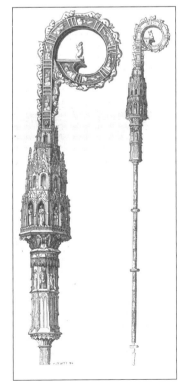

A larger version of Wykeham's actual tomb and monument from Edward Blore's *Monumental Remains of Noble and Eminent Persons* of 1826. The artist is Blore himself and the engraver Henry Le Keux. The engraving itself is dated 29 September 1825 (135x190).

The chantry of Bishop William of Waynflete, the founder of Magdalen College, Oxford and in the background on the left the chantry of Cardinal Beaufort. The artist is Edward Blore and the engraver John Le Keux. The engraving is dated 1 September 1817 and comes from John Britton's *Cathedral Antiquities* (155x215).

A further view of Waynflete's chantry. The artist is Richard Hamilton Essex and the engravers are Joseph Skelton and James Tingle. The engraving comes from Skelton"s *Pietas Oxoniensis* of 1828, although it is actually dated 1 February 1829

A representation of William of Waynflete from a cast in the library of Magdalen College, Oxford. The artist is C. Grant and the engravers are Joseph Skelton and James Fittler. The engraving comes from Skelton's *Pietas Oxoniensis* of 1828, but is dated 1 June 1830 (230x175).

A view of Bishop Richard Fox's chantry. Fox and Hugh Odiham, Bishop of Exeter, were joint founders of Corpus Christi College, Oxford. The artist is Richard Hamilton Essex and the engravers are Joseph Skelton and Henry Winkles. The engraving comes from Skeltons *Pietas Oxoniensis* of 1828 and is dated more exactly 1 May 1828 (270x190).

The elaborate gothic monument to Bishop Wilberforce designed by Sir George Gilbert Scott in 1874. It comes from the *Building News* and is dated 25 December 1874 and was photolithographed and printed by James Akerman and Co., but surely even the most Scrooge-like employer could not have had their employees work on Christmas Day? (280x175).

A view embracing Cardinal Beaufort's chantry in the centre, part of Bishop Fox's chantry on the left and Bishop Waynflete's in the background between the two. The artist is Edward Blore and the engraver Edmund Turrell. The date is 1 September 1817 and the engraving comes from John Britton's *Cathedral Antiquities* (155x200).

The Deanery was in medieval times the Prior's lodging and parts of the building date from the thirteenth century. This sketch with the Cathedral in the background is by S.J. Newman and was photolithoed by James Akerman. It appeared in the *Building News* of 17 September 1886 (175x275).

A drawing of the Deanery from *Picturesque Memorials of Winchester* of 1830 by Owen Browne Carter. The engraver is John Le Keux (100x140).

A sketch of the Deanery by George Herbert Kitchen from the *Builder* of 1 October 1892 (154x180).

Cheyney Court consists of three gabled timber framed houses, which until 1888 had plastered fronts. They are in the Close by St Swithun's Gate, that can just be seen on the extreme right of the sketch. It is dated August 1888 and signed with a monogram in which a capital letter L predominates. From the *Builder* of 1 October 1892 (136x185).

Cheyney Court as seen by Herbert Railton in a drawing from *Our English Minsters* of 1893 by Frederic William Farrar, Dean of Canterbury (125x90).

A sketch of Cheyney Court by Charles G. Harper from *Royal Winchester* of 1889 by the Reverend A.G. L'Estrange (65x80).

Cheyney Court still with its plastered fronts. A sketch by Joseph Pennell from Mrs Schuyler Van Rensselaer's *English Cathedrals* of 1887. The engraver is M. Jones (75x103).

A line drawing also by Joseph Pennell entitled simply 'In the Close' from Mrs Schuyler Van Rensselaer's *English Cathedrals* of 1887 (72x116).

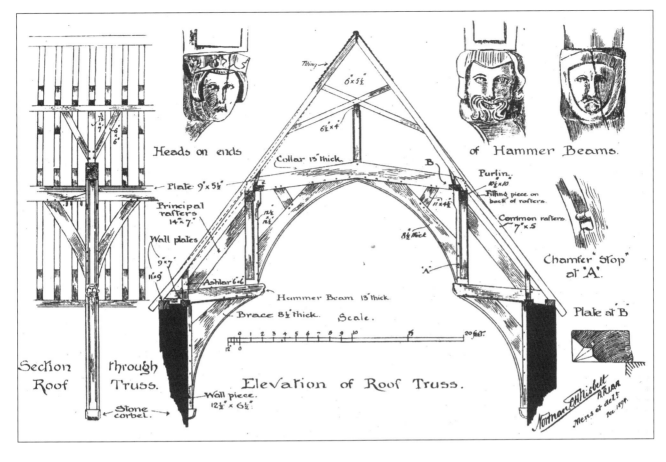

Pilgrims were the back-packers of the middle ages and swarmed all over Europe and the Near East to earn merit from visiting the shrines of notable saints. A good relic brought these medieval tourists to your town and created prosperity, so much so that it did not do to enquire too closely into the antecedents of any particular relic or the method of its acquisition. For example the monks of Conques sent one of their brethren to Agen where he stayed as a member of the Order there for ten years and one dark night calmly filched the relics of the female Saint Foy. He then took them back to Conques where the veneration of the saint made the village a major stopping point on the way to the shrine of St James at Compostela. In the Close at Winchester the Pilgrims' Hall was constructed in the fourteenth century to house those pilgrims who were coming to venerate the shrine of St Swithun in the Cathedral. It has the earliest hammerbeam roof so far identified and since 1931 has formed part of Pilgrims School, which was founded at that date as a combined choir and preparatory school. Above are details of the roof dated December 1894 and the artist is Norman C.H. Nisbett. The drawing comes from the *Proceedings of the Hampshire Field Club and Archaeological Society* of the same year (120x190). Below an undated but Edwardian view of the roof trusses from the *Pilgrims' Way From Winchester to Canterbury*, which although later published in book form started life as articles in the *Art Journal* of 1892 by Julia Cartwright. The black cat stalking the two mice or rats adds a touch of drama to the scene. The artist is Alexander Murray (75x100).

A view of the exterior of the Pilgrims' Hall. The artist is Norman C.H. Nisbett and the date December 1894. It comes from the *Proceedings of the Hampshire Field Club and Archaeological Society* (120x190).

EPISCOPAL PALACES
AND FOUNDATIONS

The Bishops of Winchester from medieval times onwards might well be described as keen patrons of the building trade. Not only did they carry out extensive work on their own cathedral, but supervised the construction of palaces, residences, colleges, schools, almshouses and, before the Reformation, monastic foundations. One Bishop, Godfrey de Lucy (1189-1204), even set up a planned town at New Alresford, dammed a river to form a reservoir and treated himself to a small palace there for good measure. Many of these foundations have disappeared with hardly a trace, but a large number survive in a very flourishing state. In Winchester alone in addition to the Cathedral, there are Winchester College and St Cross, while three Oxford Colleges, New, Magdalen and Corpus Christi owe their original existence to Bishops William of Wykeham (1367-1404), William Waynflete (1447-1486) and Richard Fox (1500-1528).

Perhaps however the most outstanding medieval foundation was Winchester Palace, built on land once part of Bermondsey Abbey close to the present Southwark Cathedral. If it still existed the nearest parallels would be Lambeth or Fulham Palaces, but all that remains of this extensive set of buildings and grounds is the tracery of one exquisite rose window, high up in a wall that was part of a great hall gutted by fire in 1814. Its founder was Bishop William Giffard (1100-1129), who also created Waverley Abbey in Surrey and at this point it is as well to remember that many of the bishops were not just responsible for the organisation of their diocese, but also held high offices of state and needed to be close to government. One considerable bonus that sprang from the ownership of the Palace and its surrounding area was the vast amount of revenue, that accrued to the Diocese from the enterprises carried on in the Liberty of the Clink in which this complex of buildings was situated. For the most part, these enterprises would not have been tolerated within the confines of the City of London itself, as they consisted of brothels, prisons, theatres, bear baiting pits, the less appealing trades and low life generally. Eventually various part of the buildings of the Palace began to be used for commercial purposes, a process accelerated by the fire of 1814 and the very word 'clink' became a general slang term for prison. Thereafter in London came an episcopal residence in Chelsea, roughly at the northern end of the present Albert Bridge near the junction of the eastern part of Cheyne Walk and Oakley Street, and then a town house in St James's Square.

Until 1927 when the Dioceses of Guildford and Portsmouth were carved out of that of Winchester, the principal episcopal residence was Farnham Castle. In that year it passed to the Bishop of Guildford and over a thousand years of ownership of the estate by the Diocese of Winchester ended. Farnham had been a real castle up to the Civil War with a turbulent history, but after that date gradually became a very comfortable residence. After 1927 it could be said that the Bishop of Winchester came home when he began to reside at Wolvesey.

Two other episcopal residences were at Esher and Bishops' Waltham. A tiny part of the former still survives in the gatehouse and Cardinal Wolsey when Bishop of Winchester (an appointment honoured in the breach rather than the observance) was banished there briefly before his final demise. Bishops' Waltham was built on a fairly grand scale by Henry de Blois, but suffered badly in the Civil War, fell into ruin and is now in the hands of English Heritage. De Blois was also responsible in Winchester itself for Wolvesey Castle and St Cross.

Abbeys and priories rarely survived intact at the Dissolution although the monastic church was sometimes taken over by the people of the locality for their own worship. More often the whole monastic complex was looked on as a handy source of cut stone for a private mansion or building in the area generally. This fate was suffered by the three monastic foundations of Peter de Roches (1204-1228), Titchfield, Selborne and Halesowen. Titchfield was originally converted into a house by Sir Thomas Wriothesley, the first Earl of Southampton, but was dismantled in 1781, Selborne Priory has only been recovered by excavation, while the remnants of the buildings of Halesowen Abbey are now mixed up with the installations of a farm.

Two interesting foundations in Winchester itself have also disappeared while the gatehouse of a third, Hyde Abbey, still survives. The first of these two was the Hospital of St Mary Magdalen, the work of Bishop Toclive (1174-1188) which was demolished in the late eighteenth century, but a Norman doorway survived to be incorporated into the Roman Catholic church in St Peter's Street. There are however two large views of the interior of the institution's chapel (each 315x450) drawn by Jacob Schnebbelie and engraved by James Basire in *Vetusta Monumenta*, one of the publications of the Society of Antiquaries. Both views are dated 23 April 1790. The second was the College of St Elizabeth of Hungary just south of Wolvesey founded by John de Pontissara (1282-1304) in 1300. It lasted to the Dissolution when it was granted to Sir Thomas Wriothesley who promptly sold it on to Winchester College at a profit with the proviso that it be retained as a grammar school or demolished. In the event it suffered the latter fate and also the further indignity of having parts of its fabric used to construct a wall. Thus perished an institution dedicated to the patron saint of queens.

Finally mention should be made of Bishop William Edington (1346-1366) who in his native village in Wiltshire founded a College of Bonhommes, an unusual foundation of friars who followed the rule of St Augustine. As befitted a person who played a highly significant part in the building of Winchester Cathedral, he also rebuilt the church at Edington in the decade between 1352 and 1361 to serve both his new foundation and the village generally. Although the College perished at the Dissolution the church at Edington remains as one of the most perfect and complete examples of the transition from decorated to perpendicular, not only in Wiltshire, but in the whole country.

Wenceslaus Hollar was a native of Prague, who as an engraver worked in Germany and Holland before coming to England with Thomas Howard, second Earl of Arundel in 1636. Among his many commissions his 'Long View of London from Bankside' of 1647 gives a detailed drawing of the buildings along the river front and this section of the south bank shows the Palace and extensive grounds of the Bishops of Winchester at that date (this section 130x520).

How are the mighty fallen. The remains of part of the Palace by the end of the eighteenth century. This anonymous engraving comes from the *Gentleman's Magazine* of 1791 (100x165).

Two tiny views of parts of the remains of Winchester Palace sketched in 1785. They are dated 1 January 1791, although not published until 1824 in John Carter's *Specimens of Gothic Architecture* (Both 57x37).

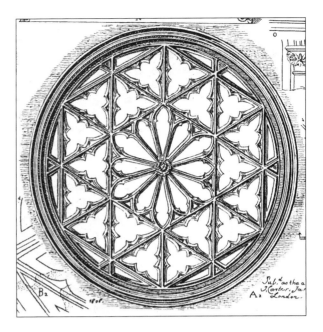

Left and above two representations of the rose window in the Great Hall of Winchester Palace, which originally measured 80 feet by 36 feet over an undercroft. This unique design of window is made up of an outer hexagon with eighteen cusped triangles surrounding a smaller hexagon filled with radiating daggers of alternating widths. It is probably fourteenth century in origin and although embowered in the nineteenth century in warehouses, by some miracle survived to be restored in 1972. On the left an etching by John Le Keux after a drawing by George Cattermole. It is dated 1 December 1822 and comes from John Britton's *Chronological History of English Architecture* (50x50). Above a drawing by John Carter from his *Ancient Architecture of England*, which is dated 1 January 1813 (85x85).

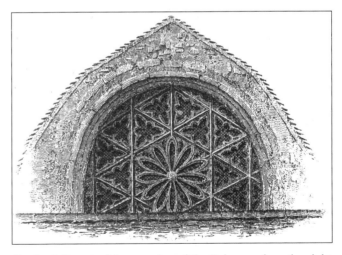

On the left part of the remains of the Palace and on the right the rose window. Both are from James Sargant Storer and John Greig's *Select Views of London and its Environs* of 1804 (ie published on a monthly basis from 1 January 1804). Both men shared the engraving and these views are by Storer and dated 1 June 1805 (left 140x115, right 80x120).

A north west view of the Great Hall of the Palace after it had been destroyed by fire on 28 August 1814. An anonymous drawing engraved by Bartholomew Howlett dated 11 April 1815. It comes from Robert Wilkinson's *Londinia Illustrata*, which started life as early as 1808 as a series of separate plates with a two volume edition in 1819 and a comprehensive edition as late as 1834 (main view 210x270, rose window 65x65).

A similar view to that above. J. Le Rous' etching from the *Beauties of Britain* of 1828 (105x175).

The rear or south view of the remains of the Palace, a much more domestic scene. Also from *Londinia Illustrata*, but dated 1 January 1812 before the fire. The artist is C.J.M. Whichelo, but no engraver is given (195x225).

A similar view to the one on the previous page, which comes from John Thomas Smith's *Antiquities of London* dated 29 September 1800. Smith was himself the artist and engraver (160x130).

A drawing by Percy Wadham of 1898, which shows nearly a century with hardly any change compared with Smith's view on the left. It comes from Walter Besant's *South London* of the same date (145x100).

A series of early views of Farnham Castle from Owen Manning's *Surrey* of 1814 drawn by John Carter and engraved by James Basire. At the top left the approach to the keep (148x105). At the top right a south-west view of the keep (122x160). Below left a south-west view of the Castle (142x215) and below right the interior looking east 'now the servants' hall' (122x146).

Later views of Farnham Castle. At the top left a sketch by Hugh Thomson from Eric Parker's *Highways & Byways in Surrey* of 1908 (105x90). At the top right a sketch by Alexander Ansted entitled 'Fox's Tower and Morley's Building' from the *Episcopal Palaces of England* of 1895 edited by Edmund Venables (120x100). At the centre and below left two views from the Art Journal of 1891 (115x150 and 65x100). Below right a further view from *Episcopal Palaces of England* entitled 'Part of the Eastern Side and Garden', also by Alexander Ansted (58x100).

Three sketches of the interior of Farnham Castle by Alexander Ansted from *Episcopal Palaces of England* of 1895 edited by Edmund Venables. Top left the entrance to the chapel (115x82), centre right a staircase (103x77) and below the dining hall (80x102).

The chapel of Wolvesey Castle from Francis Grose's *Antiquities*. The date is 6 October 1783 and the artist identified only by the initials D.L. (110x160).

The ruins of Wolvesey Castle, also from Francis Grose's *Antiquities* with the date 20 August 1783. No artist is given, but the engraver is C. Sparrow (110x160).

A view of Wolvesey Castle by Owen Browne Carter from Volume 3 of Robert Mudie's *Hampshire* of 1838. The engraver is John Le Keux and it appeared originally in Carter's *Picturesque Memorials of Winchester* of 1830 (105x150).

The same view as on the left. An anonymous wood engraving from the *Illustrated London News* of 20 September 1845 showing keen antiquarian gentlemen examining the ruins during that year's meeting of the Archaeological Institute in Winchester (110x155).

Details of the ruins of Wolvesey Castle. All except those below left are from the *Proceedings* of the Archaeological Institute's meeting at Winchester in 1845. The artist is Owen Browne Carter and the engravers Philip Henry Delamotte and John Smith Heaviside (top left 70x95, top right 35x78, centre right 60x88, below right 38x75). The ruins below left are by John Adey Repton and the engraver is James Basire. They are dated 23 April 1809 and come from the Society of Antiquaries' publication *Archaeologia* (150x100).

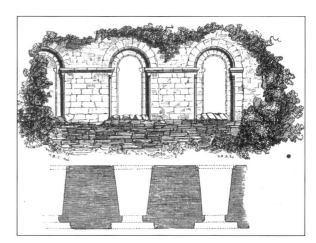

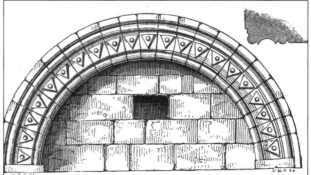

Wolvesey House is the present residence of the Bishops of Winchester dating from 1684 and stands next to the ruins of Wolvesey Castle. The view at the top is from Thomas Warton's *History and Antiquities* of Winchester of 1793. The artist is W. Cave and the engraver James Taylor (65x130).

A further view by H. Inigo Triggs from John Belcher and Mervyn Macartney's *Later Renaissance Architecture in England* of 1901 showing building modifications (90x220).

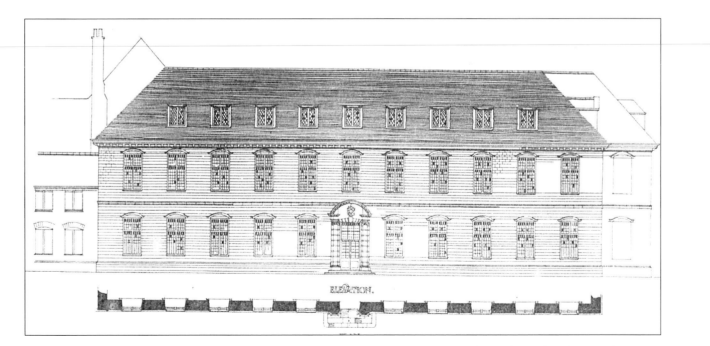

An almost similar view to the one above by L.G. Detmar dated 1902 from Volume 6 of the third series of the *Architectural Association's Sketch Books* (280x380).

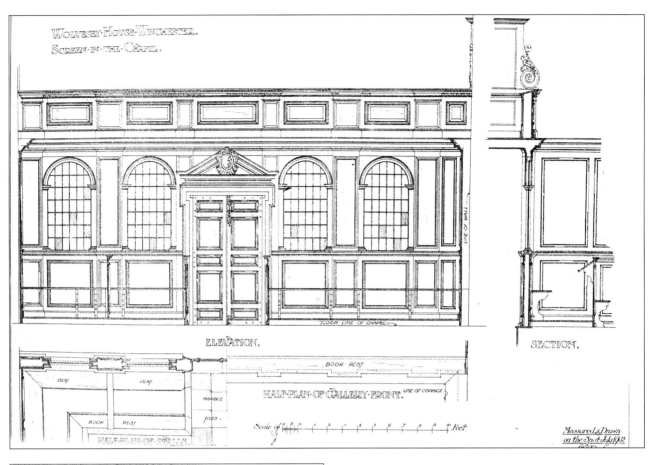

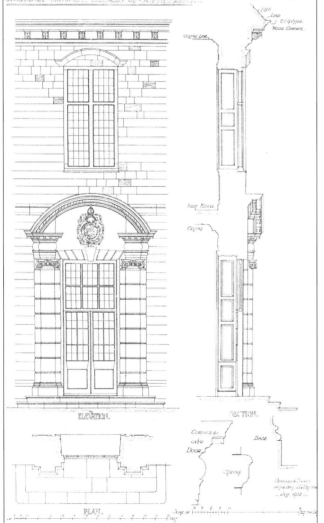

Two measured drawings of Wolvesey, also by L.G. Detmar from Volume 6 of the third series of the *Architectural Association's Sketch Books*. That at the top is entitled 'Screen in the Chapel', while the one below has details of the south front (top 280x395, below 390x280).

Esher Palace was founded by Bishop Waynflete and although later made into a private residence in the eighteenth century with William Kent as architect, all that now remains is the gatehouse. This is known variously as Waynflete or Wolsey's Tower, as the latter resided there briefly during his disgrace. He was nominally Bishop of Winchester in 1529-1530, an appointment honoured in the breach rather than the observance. The sketch is anonymous, the engraver simply being called Greenaway and it comes from John Timbs' *Nooks and Corners of English Life* of 1867 (125x85).

The ruins of the Palace at Bishops Waltham. It was first built by Bishop Henry de Blois in about 1175 and remained in use until being severely damaged in the Civil War, after which it was left to disintegrate. The view is by Herbert Marshall of 1893 from *Winchester College 1393-1893* by Old Wykehamists (95x145).

A sketch of the ruined Waverley Abbey by Hugh Thomson from Eric Parker's *Highways and Byways in Surrey*. The Abbey was founded by Bishop William Giffard in 1128 and was the first house of Cistercian monks in England (70x80).

A sketch of Edington Church in Wiltshire by Nelly Erichsen. It was rebuilt in his home village by Bishop William Edington between 1352 and 1361 and the sketch comes from Edward Hutton's *Highways and Byways in Wiltshire* written before the First World War, but not published until 1917 (65x95).

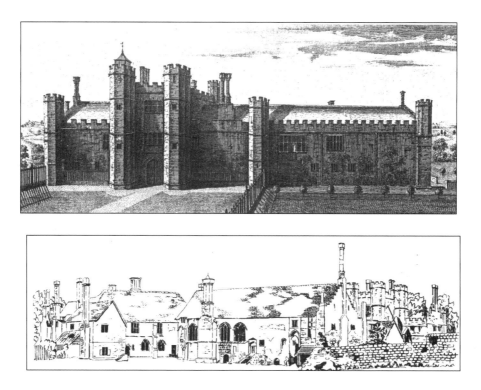

Bishop Peter de Roches founded a house of Premonstratensians at Titchfield in 1231 and at the Dissolution it was converted to a large private residence. At the top a south eastern view of Titchfield Abbey by Samuel and Nathaniel Buck from their *Antiquities*, which were issued originally in batches from 1726 onwards, the date for this particular view being 1733 (145x360). In the centre the northern aspect drawn in 1782 by Francis Grose (75x170). Below two engravings of the Abbey from Francis Grose's *Antiquities*. That on the left is dated 1761 (105x155) and on the right 1782 from the Supplement (110x155).

New College was founded in Oxford by William of Wykeham. The charter of incorporation is dated 1379 and the first occupation of the newly constructed buildings was 1386, several years ahead of Winchester College. At the top a sketch of New College by T. Raffles Davison from the *Art Journal* of 1888 (85x170), below left an engraving of the exterior of New College Chapel by John Le Keux from a drawing by Frederick Mackenzie (95x140) and below right an engraving of the interior of the Chapel, also by Le Keux and Mackenzie (140x95). Both of the latter two engravings are included in Mackenzie E.C. Walcott's *William of Wykeham and His Colleges* of 1852.

A distant view of New College with two academic gentlemen in deep conversation. An anonymous wood engraving from Mackenzie E.C. Walcott's *William of Wykeham and His Colleges* of 1852 (65x95).

A sketch by T. Raffles Davison of the Chapel Quad of New College from the *Art Journal* of 1888 (160x240).

Bishop William of Waynflete founded Magdalen College, Oxford, with a charter of incorporation of 1458. This view was engraved by J.C. Bromleny Junior for Richard Chandler's *Life of William of Waynflete* of 1811 (115x205).

Bishop Richard Fox was the joint founder with Hugh Odiham, the Bishop of Exeter, of Corpus Christi College, Oxford, in 1516. This lithograph of part of the College is by Herbert Railton and comes from Cecil Headlam's *Oxford and Its Story* of 1904 (190x170).

OTHER CHURCHES

Winchester does not have a rich variety of medieval churches, such as those existing in say Norwich and it is ironic that the two buildings dating largely from that period are just outside the real heart of the City. These are St John the Baptist in St John's Street and St Peter Chesil in Chesil Street and the irony is further compounded by the fact that the latter is now a theatre. The former villages of Hyde and Weeke, now outer parts of the City, have churches with medieval elements, but with later alterations and restorations. St Bartholomew in Hyde had two Victorian periods of restoration, while St Matthew in Weeke has seventeenth century windows. St Lawrence in Great Minster Street is in the City centre with late medieval features, but it too was restored in the Victorian period. St Michael in Kingsgate Street, in the City centre, retains a perpendicular tower, but the rest of the building is the work of William Butterfield from 1882 to 1890. Also in Kingsgate Street there is the curious little church of St Swithun, which is late medieval and forms part of the Kingsgate itself.

The rest of the story is almost wholly Victorian. Christ Church in the road of the same name is by Ewan Christian of 1861, All Saints, Petersfield Road, is by J.L. Pearson of 1890 to 1898, St Paul's, St Paul's Hill, is by the two Colsons, father and son over the long period from 1872 to 1910, St Thomas and St Clement, Southgate Street, is by E.W. Elmslie of 1845 to 1846 with a later steeple and Holy Trinity, North Walls, by Henry Woodyear of 1853 to 1854.

The Catholic church of St. Peter in St Peter's Street is of 1926 by F.A. Walters, but the shell of the former 1792 building by John Carter survives. The Congregational Church (now United Reformed) of 1853 is also in Jewry Street and is by W.F. Poulton. It appears to be one of the earliest buildings of at least a dozen produced by Poulton with his partner W.H. Woodman for the denomination all over the country, and as such therefore has a certain historical distinction.

The church of St Lawrence in Great Minster Street (the Square). The painting with a view of the church over the rooftops is by Wilfrid Williams Ball dated 1907 from *Hampshire* by the Reverend Telford Varley of 1909 (98x146).

The church of St John the Baptist which is largely perpendicular, but with a complicated building history. At the top left a view of the west end of the church by Owen Browne Carter engraved by Orlando Jewitt from the *Proceedings* of the Archaeological Institute's meeting at Winchester in 1845 (67x95). At the top right a sketch from the same angle by Charles G. Harper from the Reverend A.G. L'Estrange's *Royal Winchester* of 1889. The chimney on the left of the central window presumably meant that a heating system had been fitted since the 1845 view (65x90). Centre an east view by W.B. Roberts from A.R. Bramston and A.C. Leroy's *City of Memories* of 1893. The tip of the chimney of the heating system appears just above the centre of the roofline (85x150). Below the original entrance to the roof loft 'traced by J.Q. from a drawing by W.G.' Even the tatty yellowing pieces of paper on the notice board are faithfully reproduced. From the *Builder* of 5 December 1908 (140x125).

Various details of St John's Church by Owen Browne Carter and engraved by Orlando Jewitt, Philip Henry Delamotte and John Smith Heaviside. At the top left bench ends (60x35 and 68x20). At the top right the Easter sulpulchre and altar tomb (73x75) and centre left the very fine thirteenth century window of the south chapel (72x56). Centre right the sedila and piscina. Below left the central screen, also by Carter, Delamotte and Heaviside, all from the *Proceedings* of the Archaeological Institute's meeting at Winchester of 1845. Below right the church's consecration cross drawn by F.J. Baigent and dated 3 August 1853, but not published until 1884 (82x82).

The Church of St Peter Cheesehill or Chesil, a mixture of decorated and perpendicular, which was converted into a theatre in the 1960s. At the top a view by Owen Browne Carter engraved by John Le Keux for Carter's *Picturesque Memorials of Winchester* of 1830. A number of people are going about their everyday business on the unsurfaced road of the period (110x150). Below a drawing by Charles G. Harper from the Reverend A.G. L'Estrange's *Royal Winchester* of 1889 (107x87).

Further views of St Peter Chesil. At the top an early drawing by the architect Maurice B. Adams from a sketch made during an excursion by the Architectural Association in August 1876. The cattle being driven through the street under the advertisement for May and Co.'s Ales and Stout give a pleasingly rural air. From the *Building News* of 20 July 1877 (140x170). Below an equally rural painting by Wilfrid Williams Ball dated 1907 from the Reverend Telford Varley's *Hampshire* of 1909 (140x105).

The war memorial at Holy Trinity Church, North Walls, an important early work of 1853 to 1854 by Henry Woodyer. It is easy to forget so long after the event, the devastating effect of the First World War and how widely it was commemorated by memorials up and down the country and throughout Europe. The design is by the architect Paul Waterhouse and comes from the *Builder* of 3 August 1917 (230x180).

At the top left the Church of St Bartholomew. It retains much Norman work in the nave, although there were two periods of rebuilding from 1857 to 1859 and again from 1879 to 1880. It was originally the village church of Hyde and this sketch by Jenny Wylie of 1908 comes from the *Victoria County History of Hampshire* of 1912 (135x100). At the top right an Early English window from St Bartholomew drawn by Owen Browne Carter and engraved by Orlando Jewitt. It comes from the *Proceedings* of the Archaeological Institute's meeting at Winchester of 1845 (75x45). Below left the Church of St Swithun which is an integral part of the Kingsgate. The gateway is fourteenth century, but much of the detailing of the church is fifteenth or sixteenth century. An anonymous sketch from the *Illustrated London News* of 19 January 1889 showing a horse and cart which has just passed through the archway of the Kingsgate (75x85). Below centre details of two of the original capitals in the Church of St Thomas. A new building by E.M. Elmslie replaced the original medieval church in 1845 to 1846. The drawing was included in the *Proceedings* of the Archaeological Institute's meeting at Winchester in 1845 and John Henry Parker comments 'It is much to be regretted that the parish have considered it necessary to destroy this interesting structure. The specimens here engraved (by Philip Henry Delamotte and John Smith Heaviside) will probably soon be the only memorial of its architectural character' (35x38 and 50x44). Below right a sundial on the Church of St. Michael, a building with a perpendicular tower, which had the north aisle removed in 1822 and a rebuild by William Butterfield in 1882 to 1890. John Henry Parker also writing in the same Archaeological Society's *Proceedings* of the 1845 meeting comments that the 1822 removal of the north aisle turned the church into a 'square preaching house'. The engravers are also Delamotte and Heaviside (35x35).

John Carter was the architect of the original Roman Catholic Church in St Peter's Street of 1792, the shell of which survives, while the present structure of 1926 was designed by F.A. Walters. At the top a view of the original interior drawn by George Sidney Shepherd and engraved by J. Shury and Son. It comes from Volume 3 of Robert Mudie's *Hampshire* of 1838 with a large family gathering of some kind taking place (105x150). Below left and right the exterior and interior of Winchester Congregational (now United Reformed) Church in Jewry Street of 1853. It is in yellow brick and one of the earliest designs of the Reading based W.F. Poulton, who with W.H. Woodman was responsible from that date for at least a dozen Congregational churches culminating in the prestigious Westminster Chapel in Buckingham Gate of 1863 to 1865. The interior is especially interesting with its forest-like roof construction. Poulton was obviously an architect with an eye to the main chance, for with a few deft touches of the draughting pen, this interior design was quite unblushingly metamorphosed into the Congregational church at St Helier in Jersey in 1854. From the *Builder* of 19 November 1853. The Winchester Church was extensively remodelled in the early 1990s (exterior 170x130, interior 160x130).

WINCHESTER COLLEGE

Life in nineteenth century English public schools was tough, but then things were tough in general. The previous century had seen cheap gin swilling around Hogarth's portraits of low life in London and the capital had also witnessed the Gordon riots. The Duke of Wellington is alleged to have made the remark that the Battle of Waterloo was won on the playing fields of Eton and also that he had no idea what one draft of recruits would do to the enemy in the Peninsular War, but they certainly terrified him.

In Winchester itself the so-called 'Swing' riots occasioned by unrest among agricultural labourers had been put down with the utmost ferocity in 1830. 137 men were transported to Australia, while a nineteen-year-old youth was hanged for committing the heinous crime of threatening a local landowner and even knocking off his hat. In the College itself there had been serious rebellions in 1793 and 1818 against generally harsh conditions and sporadic outbursts of unrest at other times. In the period from 1839 to 1843 when the buildings of New Commoners replaced Old Commoners, the then Headmaster, Dr Moberly was upbraided for having built what was termed a 'workhouse' and replied, 'My dear Sir, that is exactly what I meant to do'.

The buildings designed by the Founder, William of Wykeham remained remarkably intact until after the First World War, even allowing for the outstanding work of George Ridding between 1867 and 1870, and the whole original foundation was built on the premise of Winchester College providing a steady supply of students for New College, Oxford. Wykeham's two foundations were in reality the reverse sides of the same coin and always conceived as such. The nineteenth century curriculum of most public schools was in general an arid study of the classics backed up by sport, which was designed for training the rulers of Empire. The arts and music were considered namby-pamby

and this often led to heated discussions over the architectural merits of proposed buildings or extensions.

At Harrow the committee set up to oversee the building of Burges' flamboyant scheme for the new Speech Room resigned en bloc in the 1870s and half a century later there was much soul searching at Winchester about the exact form of a suitable war memorial. Old Wykehamists serving on the Western Front were asked their views on the subject at a somewhat surreal dinner in Amiens in 1917 prior to the Battle of Cambrai. Not surprisingly, it was not lost upon them that these views were being canvassed on a memorial to their own possible demise and those present concentrated their thoughts much more on having a thoroughly convivial evening instead. Sir Herbert Baker was eventually chosen to work on the war memorial buildings at both Harrow and Winchester in the early 1920's and the same architect was later given the commission for converting the former brewhouse into the Moberly Library from 1932 to 1934. Perhaps the most interesting of the nineteenth century work was Butterfield's remodelling of what Repton had created in Moberly and Flint Courts and Basil Champney's Memorial Building, a museum and art school, of 1898, fourteen years after his Butler Museum at Harrow. It is perhaps fair to add that the Memorial Building has not been universally admired in the period since its construction.

Any great public school will naturally have built up a formidable body of tradition in the course of its existence and it must be a source of quiet satisfaction to all Wykehamists that their College founded in 1393 was the model on which Eton was based more than half a century later. There have of course been many additions and alterations to the building stock since the First World War, which fall outside the scope of this work, but which have had a marked affect on the present layout and appearance of the College.

Not a convention of undertakers marching in procession to carry out some ancient ritual, but a nineteenth century crocodile of College boys going to 'Hills' (ie St Catherine's Hill) for their period of recreation. The artist is Philip Henry Delamotte and the engraver John Smith Heaviside. The view is included in the Reverend H.C. Adams *Wykehamica – A History of Winchester College and Commoners* of 1878 (60x110).

Two views of Wickham, the home village of William of Wykeham four miles north of Fareham. At the top a watercolour by Wilfrid Williams Ball from *Hampshire* by the Reverend Telford Varley (95x140). Below a line drawing by Herbert Marshall from *Winchester College* 1393-1893 by Old Wykehamists (80x145).

A distant view of the College from the Meads with a swan gliding peacefully past the clump of reeds. The artist is Charles Walter Radclyffe and the engraver Joseph Lionel Williams. This wood engraving is included in Mackenzie E.C. Walcott's *William of Wykeham and His Colleges* of 1852. Radclyffe produced a number of illustrated works on public schools culminating in *Memorials of Winchester College* of 1847 (85x105).

A distant view of the tower of the College chapel, juxtaposed with that shapely symbol of Victorian municipal enterprise, the chimney of the sewage works. The artist is Charles G. Harper and it comes from *Royal Winchester* by the Reverend A.G. L'Estrange of 1889 (80x90).

The College from the weirs. A sketch dated 8 April 1893 by Herbert Marshall in *Winchester College* 1393-1893 by Old Wykehamists (90x145).

A southern view of the College. A sketch by Herbert Marshall dated April 1893 from *Winchester College 1393-1893* by Old Wykehamists (105x140).

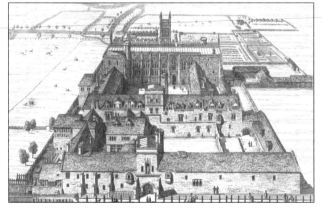

An engraving by Charles Walter Radclyffe based on David Loggan's bird's eye view of the College of 1675. The engraver is Charles' brother Edward and the illustration comes from Mackenzie E.C. Walcott's *William of Wykeham and His Colleges* of 1852 (90x140)

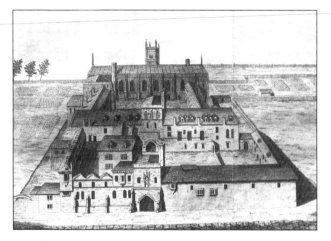

A rather cruder reworking of David Loggan's bird's eye view of the College of 1675 by W. Cave. The engraver is James Taylor and the view comes from Volume 1 of Thomas Warton's *History and Antiquities of Winchester* of 1773 (115x165).

An engraving entitled 'North East View of St Mary's College Winton' taken from outside the Warden's garden. The artist is James Cave, who worked in Winchester in the first two decades of the nineteenth century, and the engraver J. Pass. The view comes from John Milner's *History of Winchester* of 1809 (160x195).

One of the fine aquatints from Rudolph Ackermann's Public Schools and Colleges of 1816. Ackermann used some of the outstanding artists, process workers and colourists of his day to achieve the extremely high standard of his publications. The artist is William Westall and the aquatinting by Joseph C. Stadler. The view is entitled *Winchester College From the Meadow* and is dated 1 January 1815 (190x280).

Two very similar engravings from outside the Warden's garden. On the left one by Rock and Co. dated 1 July 1851 and on the right by J. Prouten of Winchester, the engraver being Newman and Company. In the Rock and Co. view it appears that the roof of the chapel has been left out and one can only speculate that this was the result of the anonymous engraver resuming work after a particularly good lunch (Rock & Co. 60x90, J. Prouten 80x145).

This view comes from *City of Memories* of 1893 by A.R. Bramston and A.L. Leroy. The artist is W.B. Roberts (70x155).

A sketch by Herbert Marshall entitled 'The College From Wolvesey Gate' from almost the same viewpoint as the one above. It comes from *Winchester College 1393-1893* by Old Wykehamists (125x177).

Three views from the Warden's garden. At the top a wood engraving by Joseph Lionel Williams after an original drawing by Charles Walter Radclyffe from Mackenzie E.C. Walcott's *William of Wykeham and His Colleges* of 1852 (90x90). The engraving at the centre is by J. Sadler after J. Clarke Armytage from Volume 1 of Bernard Bolingbroke Woodward's *General History of Hampshire* of 1861 to 1869 (140x195). Below is an anonymous wood engraving from the *Illustrated London News* of January 31 1891 (80x150).

A view entitled 'College Tower, Library and Mill' by Owen Browne Carter from his *Picturesque Memorials* of Winchester of 1830. The engraver is William Tombleson who also engraved and published works on the Thames and Rhine after his own paintings (135x100).

An aquatint by Joseph C. Stadler from a drawing by William Westall entitled 'Winchester College from the Warden's Garden'. It comes from Rudolph Ackermann's *Public Schools and Colleges* of 1816 and makes an interesting comparison with the work from the same source on page 120. It is dated 1 January 1816 (180x270).

Three views of parts of the College chapel. At the top left a drawing by G.H. Shepherd, which was engraved by J. Shury and Son for Volume 3 of Robert Mudie's *Hampshire* of 1838. Either this is an obscure member of the extensive Shepherd family of topographical artists or the H. is a mistake for S, as many of the other drawings in Mudie's work are by George Sidney Shepherd (155x110). At the top right a sketch by T. Raffles Davison from the *Art Journal* of 1888 (190x125). Bottom, a drawing by Charles G. Harper from *Royal Winchester* of 1889 by the Reverend A.G. L'Estrange (140x100).

Four views of the outer gateway of the College. At the top left a drawing by Owen Browne Carter from his *Picturesque Memorials of Winchester* of 1830 engraved by John Le Keux (110x135). At the top right an anonymous wood engraving from the *Illustrated London News* of 31 January 1891 (75x75). At the centre a drawing by Samuel Williams from the second edition of Samuel Howitt's *Visits to Remarkable Places* of 1888 (56x75). Below a sketch by William B. Robinson from Philip W. Sergeant's *Cathedral Church of Winchester* of 1898 (100x60). In the centre of the gate tower is an impressive statue of the Virgin Mary contemporary with the original construction, as it is to Her that the College is dedicated and this statue is clearly visible in all four illustrations.

Three further views of the outer gateway to the College, all of 1893. Two are by Herbert Marshall from *Winchester College 1393-1893* by Old Wykehamists. The one at the top left is entitled 'Outer Gate and Warden's House' (95x145), while that below is entitled simply 'College Street' (145x190). The third at the top right is by W.B. Roberts from *City of Memories* by A.R. Bramston and A.C. Leroy (115x115).

An aquatint dated 1 February 1816 and entitled 'Winchester College Entrance with the Warden's House' from Rudolph Ackermann's *Public Schools and Colleges* of 1816. The artist is William Westall and the aquatinting by Daniel Havell (245x215).

The very handsome Chamber court and gateway. At the top a sketch by Charles G. Harper from the Reverend A.G. L'Estrange's *Royal Winchester* of 1889 (145x135). Below right a drawing by Herbert Marshall from *Winchester College 1393-1893* by Old Wykehamists (135x90). Centre left another sketch entitled 'Middle Gate' from the same source (145x150). Below left a painting by Wilfrid Williams Ball from the Reverend Telford Varley's *Hampshire* of 1909 (115x145).

At the top a drawing of the latin speech 'Ad Portas', which was given at the Middle Gate to greet the electors from New College, who joined an equal number of electors from Winchester College to decide the face of candidates (or candlesticks) for admission. The drawing is by Henry Garland from Robert Mansfield's *School Life at Winchester* of 1863. Mansfield talks of Garland's work in less than glowing terms when he writes in the preface 'The other pictures by Mr. Garland sufficiently well represent the architectural features of the College, but justice is scarcely done to the figures of boys, who do not go through their labours and amusements in such rigid style as might be inferred from their figures and attitudes here represented' (80x135). Below one of Herbert Marshall's sketches from *Winchester College 1393-1893* by Old Wykehamists. It is entitled 'View from Moberly's Court' (200x145).

'School and Tower' is the title of Herbert Marshall's sketch at the top (55x40). At the centre another entitled 'School and Tower from Meads' (145x200). The former depicts the side of School and the latter the rear with a leisurely cricket match in progress. Both are from *Winchester School 1393-1893* by Old Wykehamists. Below an anonymous drawing which appears stylistically to be by William B. Robinson from Philip Sergeant's *Cathedral Church of Winchester* of 1898. It shows the tower and the back of School (65x87).

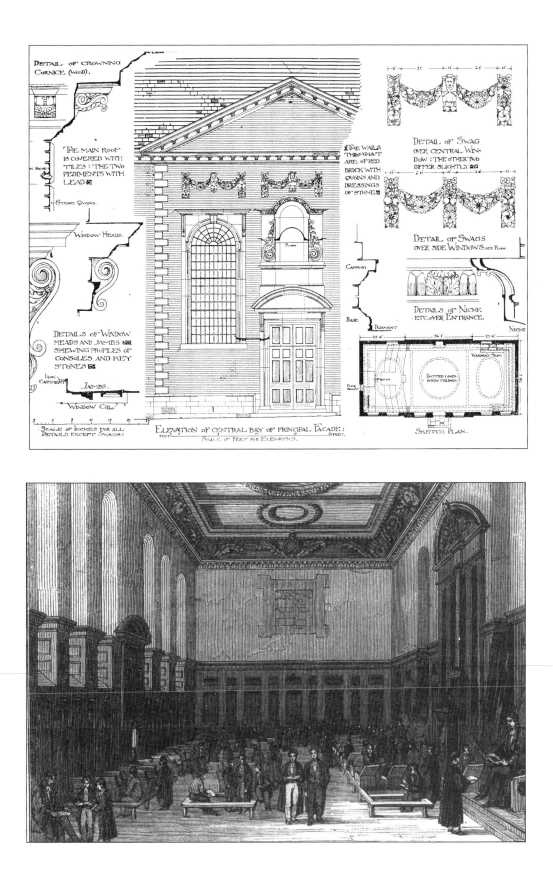

At the top the elegant front of School built between 1683 and 1687. The doubtful attribution to Sir Christopher Wren is a triumph of contemplation over documentation. In addition to the fine garlands there is a statue of William of Wykeham of 1692 in the central niche (not shown here) by Caius Gabriel Cibber, who was responsible for the phoenix above the south porch of St Paul's Cathedral. The drawing comes from John Belcher and Mervyn Macartney's *Later Renaissance Architecture in England* of 1901 (300x405). Below the equally elegant interior of School, which although of a much higher standard of decoration, bears a close resemblance to the interior of the Old Schools at Harrow. The artist is Charles Walter Radclyffe and the wood engraving comes from Mackenzie E.C. Walcott's *William of Wykeham and His Colleges* of 1862 (70x95).

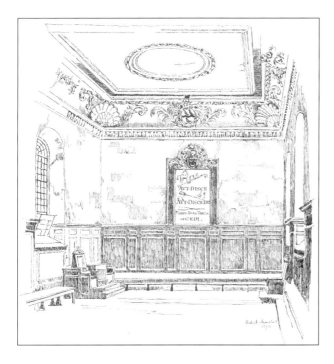

At the top left Herbert Marshall's view of the interior of School from *Winchester College 1393-1893* by Old Wykehamists. The framed wording on the far wall in latin can be translated as 'Learn and you can obtain a bishop's mitre – go away and become a soldier, author or lawyer – if neither course appeals, stay and be beaten' (155x145). At the top right the seat of power in School with the instruments of punishment. An anonymous drawing from the Reverend H.C. Adams' *Wykehamica – A History of Winchester College and Commoners* of 1878 (47x55). Below a drawing of School by Henry Garland from Robert Mansfield's *School Life at Winchester College* of 1863. Punishment is clearly in the offing on the right (80x135).

At the top an anonymous wood engraving from the *Illustrated London News* of 22 June 1861 entitled 'Winchester College Schoolroom' (160x235). Below 'Domum', as seen by another anonymous artist, also from the *Illustrated London News*, but of 22 July 1884 (150x235). This week of celebrations at the end of the summer term has gradually been whittled down to more manageable proportions since the Victorian heyday depicted here.

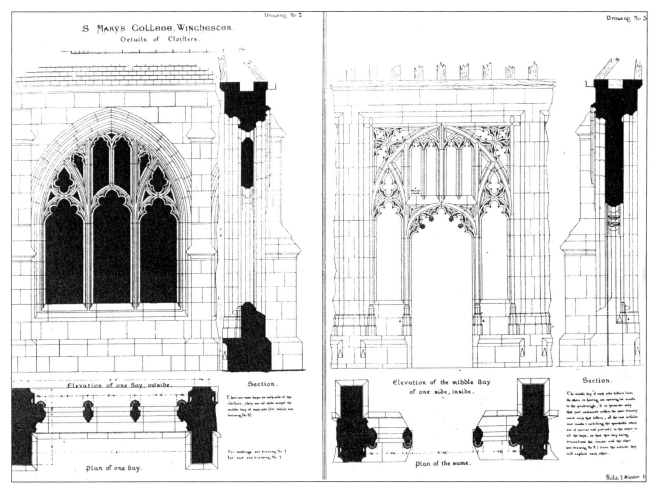

Detailed drawings of parts of the Cloisters by Philip J. Marvin of 1873. They come from Volume 5 of the New Series of the *Architectural Association's Sketch Books* (top 270x380, below 260x380).

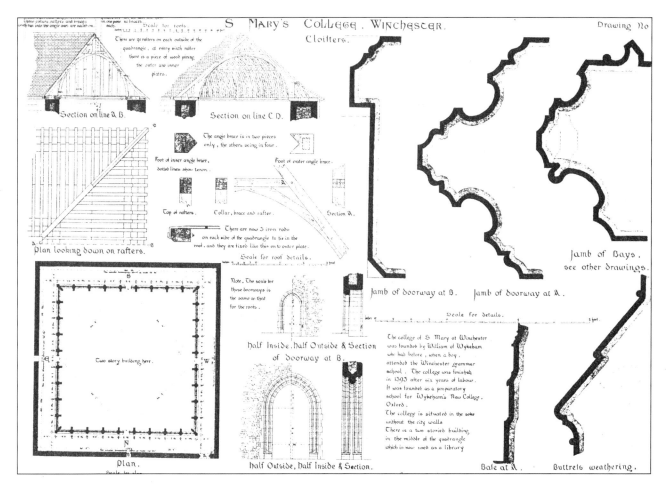

At the top left a view in the Cloisters by Herbert Marshall from *Winchester College 1393-1893* by Old Wykehamists (205x135). At the top right the Memorial gateway to General Herbert Stewart of 1885 by George Frederick Bodley, which now leads to New Hall. Stewart was a Wykehamist who had attained the rank of Major General and lost his life fighting in the Sudan. There is also a monument to him in St Paul's Cathedral. An anonymous wood engraving from the *Illustrated London News* of 31 January 1891 (75x50). Below a sketch of a corner of the Cloisters by Charles G. Harper from *Royal Winchester* of 1889 by the Reverend A.G. L'Estrange (95x135).

The Cloisters.

At the top the west walk of the Cloisters. A wood engraving by Charles Walter Radclyffe from Mackenzie E.C. Walcott's *William of Wykeham and His Colleges* of 1852. The engraver is Joseph Lionel Williams and the figure is in the original dress of a scholar (80x100). Below a drawing by Herbert Marshall of part of the Cloisters and the entrance to Fromond's Chantry. This latter is a fifteenth - century structure of Bere stone consecrated in 1437 to the memory of John Fromond, a Steward of the Manors, who left money for its construction. Fromond was a genial soul and a great trencherman, who for many years did not draw his salary and was thus a great favourite with the College authorities. For some two hundred and fifty years until 1895 the Chantry was used as a library, but at that date was converted back into use as a chapel for the younger boys. In 1924 the upper floor of this beautiful building was converted into a not very accessible art room. From *Winchester College 1393-1893* by Old Wykehamists (200x140).

At the top left part of the Cloisters and Fromond's Chantry. The artist is Wilfrid Williams Ball and the painting comes from the Reverend Telford Varley's *Hampshire* of 1909 (140x110). At the top right the entrance to Fromond's Chantry. The artist is William B. Robinson and the drawing comes from Philip W. Sergeant's *Cathedral Church of Winchester* of 1898 (90x96). Two views of the College Sick House, an attractive seventeenth century building. Centre one of Herbert Marshall's sketches from *Winchester College 1393-1893* by Old Wykehamists (110x140). Below right an anonymous wood engraving from the *Illustrated London News* of 31 January 1891 (45x72). Additional accommodation for those who become ill is provided by a sanatorium completed in 1893 by the architect William White.

Two views of parts of the Second Master's house. At the top a drawing by Herbert Marshall from *Winchester College 1393-1893* by Old Wykehamists (125x140). Top right a painting by Wilfrid Williams Ball from the Reverend Telford Varley's *Hampshire* of 1909 (140x110). Below left a part of the former brewhouse, which dates from the days of medieval self-sufficiency and was converted into a section of the Moberly Library by Sir Herbert Baker between 1932 and 1934. The drawing is anonymous, but by style probably by Charles Walter Radclyffe and is from Mackenzie E.C. Walcott's *William of Wykeham and His Colleges* of 1852 (90x90). Below right a painting by Wilfrid Williams Ball from the Reverend Telford Varley's *Hampshire* of 1909 (140x110).

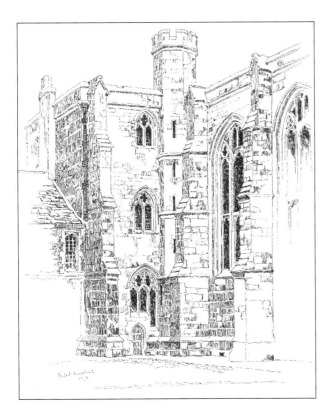

Four views of the exterior of the Chapel from Chamber Court. At the top left a sketch by Herbert Marshall from *Winchester College 1393-1893* by Old Wykehamists (175x155). Top right and below two etchings by W.B. Roberts entitled respectively 'Morning Chapel' and 'Evening Chapel', which come from *City of Memories* by A.R. Bramston and A.C. Leroy of 1893 (both 95x145). Bottom a drawing by Charles Walter Radclyffe from Mackenzie E.C. Walcott's *William of Wykeham and His Colleges* of 1852. The engraver is Charles' brother Edward (85x140).

At the top an aquatint of the exterior of the Chapel from Rudolph Ackermann's *Public Schools and Colleges* of 1816. The artist is William Westall and the aquatinting by J. Bluck. The exact date of the aquatint is 1 February 1816 (200x255). Below left a sketch of the exterior of the Chapel by T. Raffles Davison from the *Art Journal* of 1888 (100x145). Below right an anonymous wood engraving also of the exterior of the Chapel from the *Illustrated London News* of January 31 1891 (70x100).

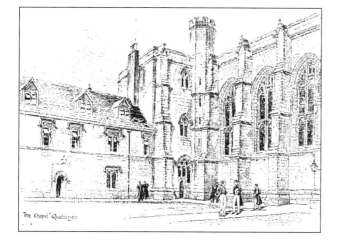

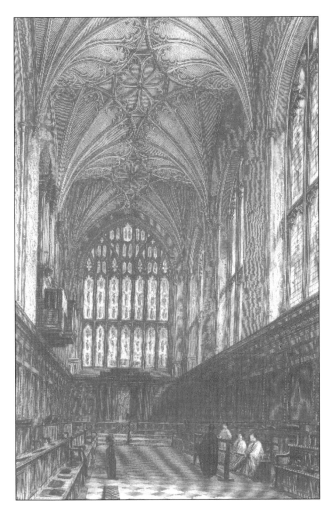

At the top left the interior of the Chapel before William Butterfield's restoration of 1874-1875. One of the outstanding features is the cusped lierne vault. Butterfield removed much of the 1680s woodwork, most of which after many vicissitudes surfaced again to be incorporated into the New Hall at the end of the 1950s. This engraving comes from Mackenzie E.C. Walcott's *William of Wykeham and His Colleges* of 1852. The artist is Charles Walter Radclyffe and the engraver his brother Edward (135x90). Above right the consecration cross of the Chapel from a drawing dated 11 December 1874 by Francis Joseph Baigent and published ten years later (65x65). Below anonymous drawings of some of the painted glass in the Chapel showing the glass painter (87x30) and mason, carpenter, and clerk of works (62x105) who worked on the building. From the *Proceedings* of the Archaeological Institute's meeting at Winchester in 1845.

The misericords of the choir stalls in the Chapel, which escaped destruction or removal by William Butterfield during his restoration of 1874-1875. The lithographs are by Emma Phipson from her book *Choir Stalls and Their Carving* of 1896. Starting from the top downwards, a falcon with a mallard in its talons flanked by leaves (60x150), a dragon with strongly marked ribs and foliage (65x165), a lion's mouth with protruding tongue and two dragons curled in circles (60x160), a cripple with clogs on hands and knees with feet like hands, accompanied by a man in a hat and long cloak brandishing a falchion and an ape in a hood and tight-fitting jester's dress with a horn (70x180), a countryman with hat tied under his chin with laced boots and a sheep under each arm accompanied by the Good Shepherd and a man in a hood standing on a spray of convolvulus (65x170), finally a human headed dragon with outspread wings flanked by foliage (65x160).

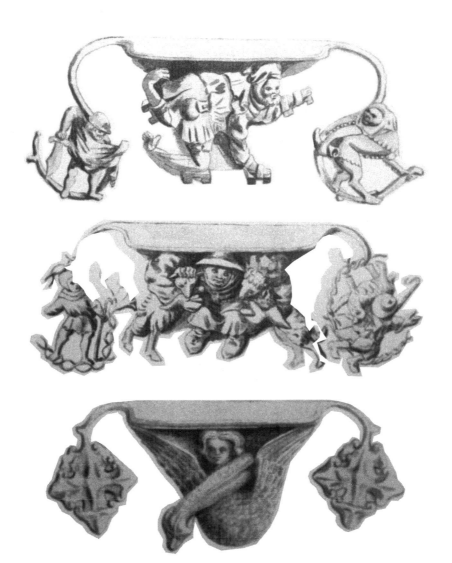

The Trusty Servant.

A PIECE OF ANTIQUITY

Painted on the wall adjoining to the kitchen of Winchester College.

A TRUSTY SERVANT'S PORTRAIT WOULD YOU SEE,
THIS EMBLEMATIC FIGURE WELL SURVEY,
THE PORKER'S SNOUT NOT NICE IN DIET SHEWS,
THE PADLOCK SHUT NO SECRETS HE'LL DISCLOSE,
PATIENT THE ASS HIS MASTER'S WRATH WILL BEAR,
SWIFTNESS IN ERRAND THE STAG'S FEET DECLARE,
LOADED HIS LEFT HAND APT TO LABOUR SAITH,
THE VEST HIS NEATNESS OPEN HAND HIS FAITH.
GIRT WITH HIS SWORD HIS SHIELD UPON HIS ARM,
HIMSELF & MASTER HE'LL PROTECT FROM HARM.

At the top left a meal in Hall. An anonymous wood engraving from the *Illustrated London News* of 31 January 1891 (150x100). At the top right one end of the Hall as sketched by Herbert Marshall in *Winchester College 1393-1893* by Old Wykehamists (205x130). Below the so-called Trusty Servant. An undated anonymous engraving by Rock and Co. The picture hangs in the Buttery adjoining the College kitchen (servant only 115x105, servant with explanatory verse 180x105).

Top left the latin canticle 'Domum' being sung in Hall. A wood engraving from Mackenzie E.C. Walcott's *William of Wykeham and His Colleges* of 1852. The artist is Charles Walter Radclyffe and the engraver Joseph Lionel Williams. It was re-used in the Reverend H.C. Adams' *Wykehamica – A History of Winchester College and Commoners* of 1878 (100x90). Top right a corner of the Hall from the *English Illustrated Magazine* of 1890/1891. The artist is William Harold Oakley, who also practised as an architect (200x90). Below a rather vigorous breakfast in Hall from Robert Mansfield's *School Life at Winchester College*. That on the right is from the third edition of 1893 and the artist is Henry Garland. In the first edition of 1863 the scholars on the left and the gentleman wielding the cane are top-hatted, but the effluxion of time between the editions means that their headgear has been rather strangely removed (130x78).

The Audit Room which lies above the Buttery and Pantry near a corner of the Hall was originally used for the annual audit of the College estates. It has a fine beamed ceiling supported on stone corbels and an early tiled floor. The tapestries shown in the illustration below were removed to the Hall and the armour above the door has also been removed. At the top a sketch by Herbert Marshall from *Winchester College 1393-1893* by Old Wykehamists (130x145). Below an anonymous wood engraving from the *Illustrated London News* of June 22 1861, which has the curious air of a rather austere men's club a long way from Pall Mall (150x230).

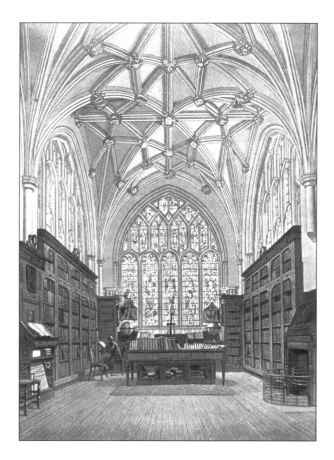

Until 1875 Fromond's Chantry in the centre of the Cloisters was used as a library and it is so shown in the above illustrations. After that date it was converted back to religious uses and serves as a chapel for the younger boys of the College. At the top left an aquatint from Rudolph Ackermann's *Public Schools and Colleges* of 1816. The artist is Frederick Mackenzie and the aquatintist W.J. Bennett (260x90). At the top right an anonymous wood engraving from Mackenzie E.C. Walcott's *William of Wykeham and His Colleges* of 1852 entitled simply 'Library Door' (90x90). Below left the Sixth Chamber in 1893 where the Prefect of Hall (the Head Boy of the College) presided. A sketch by Herbert Marshall from *Winchester College 1393-1893* by Old Wykehamists (155x170). Below right the Election Chamber where boys learned their fate, whether in the first instance they would be admitted to Winchester College or later to New College in Oxford. A wood engraving from Mackenzie E.C. Walcott's *William of Wykeham and His Colleges* of 1852. The artist is Charles Walter Radclyffe and the engraver Joseph Lionel Williams (80x100).

At the top is William Butterfield's Crimean War Memorial of 1858, which is situated near the entrance to the Chapel. The artist is Henry Garland and the illustration is from the third edition of Robert Mansfield's *School Life at Winchester* of 1893 (130x78). Below an illustration of Sir Herbert Baker's War Memorial Cloister from the *Architectural Review* of 1924 (120x130). On the whole Baker's two war memorials of the 1920s at Harrow and Winchester, although initially criticised, have now become very much part of the architectural scene in both places. This is in contrast to his drastic remodelling of Soane's work at the Bank of England during the same period, which to many seems heavy and insensitive (160x255).

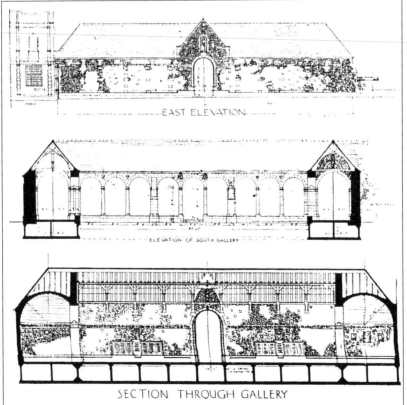

EAST ELEVATION

ELEVATION OF SOUTH GALLERY

SECTION THROUGH GALLERY

The Headmaster's House at Harrow was destroyed by fire in 1838 and replaced in 1840 by Decimus Burton. At Winchester the Headmaster's House was built between 1839 and 1842 by George Stanley Repton and both buildings are of a similarly uninspired utilitarian Victorian Gothic. This wood engraving of the house by Orlando Jewitt is from a drawing by Philip Henry Delamotte in the Reverend H.C. Adams' *Wykehamica – A History of Winchester College* of 1878 (85x105).

Basil Champneys' Quincentenary Memorial Museum building completed in 1897, that in its boldness should be compared with the very different, but equally bold, Butler Museum and Schools of 1886 by the same architect at Harrow. During the 1890s Champneys was largely engaged on the John Rylands Library in Manchester. The illustration is from the *Builder* of 16 November 1895 (220x380).

A view of Old Commoners built between 1739 and 1742. This unlovely and unloved building was replaced exactly a century later by New Commoners, equally unloved and dubbed a 'workhouse', and itself superseded by other buildings in 1869. An anonymous wood engraving from Mackenzie E.C. Walcott's *William of Wykeham and His Colleges* of 1862 (70x100).

The 'New Field' was obtained by George Ridding during his Headship (1867-1870), initially at his own expense. It provides a magnificent setting for many cricket matches, especially those against outside teams, although Meads and Lavender Meads are still also used. At the top a view of New Field showing the thatched 'Webbe Tent' later replaced by the 'Hunter Tent'. The sketch is by Herbert Marshall and comes from *Winchester College 1393-1893* by Old Wykehamists (105x200). Below the match against Eton on the Meads in 1864. An anonymous wood engraving from the *Illustrated London News* of 9 July 1864 (170x235).

At the top another view of cricket on the Meads. An anonymous wood engraving from the *Illustrated London News* of 31 January 1891 (170x270). Centre and below two views of Winchester football which developed for a fearsome twenty-two-a-side scrum in the nineteenth century called a 'hot', that was definitely not for the faint-hearted into a still strenuous six-a-side version. The centre illustration of a 'hot' is by Henry Garland from the third edition of Robert Mansfield's *School Life at Winchester College* of 1893. Commoners wore red jerseys and College boys blue ones (77x130). The drawing below entitled 'Six and Six' is by Herbert Marshall from *Winchester College 1393-1893* by Old Wykehamists (200x135).

ST CROSS

St Cross is the oldest surviving almshouse in the country and was founded by Bishop Henry de Blois in about 1136. In addition to the residential accommodation there is a magnificent cruciform church begun in the twelfth century and completed in the thirteenth, the interior of which was restored by William Butterfield in 1864 to 1865, but the latter's polychromatic mural decorations have been removed since that date. The initial foundation was under the control of the Knights Hospitallers, but in 1185 became the gift of the Bishops of Winchester and had wealthy endowments. De Blois was the brother of King Stephen and in the period of anarchy during the latter's reign (1135-1154) became the principal power broker between Stephen and the Empress Matilda, veering from one side to the other in the conflict. It may seem strange at first sight that one so tough and ruthless should also have been the founder of St Cross, but De Blois in his youth had been trained at Cluny and the Cluniacs always felt they had a duty to relieve the sufferings of the poor.

The accommodation was originally for thirteen 'poor impotent men so reduced in strength as rarely or never to be able to raise themselves without the assistance of another'. In addition there was a generous form of outdoor relief, which provided one good meal a day for a hundred poor men in a part of the building called the Hundred Men's Hall. However through time abuses crept in and the foundation was reduced to dire straits. In 1445 it was refounded as a 'Hospital of Noble Poverty' by another tough and ruthless Bishop of Winchester, Cardinal Beaufort. The latter intended it as a refuge for people of rank who had fallen on hard times and the present living accommodation is almost completely work of that period. The distinction between those residents of the original foundation and that of the Cardinal still exists, as the former wear black habits with the white cross of the Knights Hospitallers, whereas the latter have red habits.

As St Cross was not a monastic foundation it escaped destruction at the time of the Dissolution, but perhaps the most scandalous period of neglect and abuse came in the first half of the nineteenth century under Brownlow North, the brother of the politician Lord North. Brownlow North was appointed Bishop of Winchester by his brother in 1781 in a neat piece of nepotism. Dr Johnson had said dismissively about Lord North that 'he fills a chair', but North was a wily politician, an attribute with which his brother was also liberally endowed, as the latter appointed his son to the wardenship of St Cross in 1808. For just under half a century the son, who was a rich man in his own right, systematically appropriated the foundation's endowments for his own use. This gross abuse was not put right until a commission of 1857 appointed proper trustees and Anthony Trollope made good use of the whole affair in his novel *The Warden*.

It is something of a miracle that St Cross has survived through the centuries as a residential almshouse and wayfarers in the shape of contemporary tourists still receive a token dole, even though none are likely to be so impotent that they cannot raise themselves without the assistance of another.

A charming view of the church at St Cross seen from the River Itchen. This engraving appears in Volume 1 of Bernard Bolingbroke Woodward's *General History of Hampshire*, which was published between 1861 and 1869. The artist is William Henry Bartlett and the engraver A. Willmore (125x192).

151

At the top a drawing by Owen Browne Carter engraved by John Le Keux. It comes from Carter's *Picturesque Memorials of Winchester* of 1830 and shows the church of St Cross and also part of Cardinal Beaufort's tower with part of the residential accommodation (105x145). At the centre an anonymous engraving of a north eastern view of the Church of St Cross included as the frontispiece in Henry Moody's *History and Description of the Hospital of St Cross* of 1840 (90x165). Below stormy skies over St Cross. The artist is George Sidney Shepherd, who was beginning to fall on hard times when this drawing was produced. It appears in Volume 3 of Robert Mudie's *Hampshire* of 1838. The engraver is J. Shury (100x150).

This view of the church of St Cross is by the Reverend John Louis Petit, an artist of Huguenot descent, from his book *Remarks on Architectural Character* of 1846 (190x320).

A very similar view to the one above by Wilfrid Williams Ball, whose painting comes from the Reverend Telford Varley's *Hampshire* of 1909 (140x100).

At the top an engraving entitled 'Church of St Cross Near Winchester' from Volume 5 of Francis Grose's *Antiquities*, which was issued originally as a part work between 1773 and 1787. As a part work it was sold by Samuel Hooper and bears the date 26 December 1783, so somebody must have had a fairly bleak Christmas. The engraver is Thomas Bonnor and Grose's original drawing is in the Society of Antiquaries Library (105x150). At the centre a drawing of the east end of the Church at St Cross by Jenny Wylie from Volume 5 of the *Victoria County History of Hampshire*. The drawing is dated 1908 and the volume 1912 (90x125). Below a sketch by Herbert Marshall entitled 'St Cross from the North' from *Winchester College 1393-1893* by Old Wykehamists (75x145).

At the top a view of the church of St Cross by John Johnson from his *Reliques of Ancient Architecture* of 1858. The lithographic firm was Day & Son and the actual lithographer A. Newman (215x315). Left, a sketch of the church of St Cross from the north west by Jenny Wylie dated 1909 from Volume 5 of the *Victoria County History of Hampshire* of 1912 (80x125). Below, a view of St Cross from the south showing part of the accommodation and also the church. The sketch is by Herbert Marshall from *Winchester College 1393-1893* by Old Wykehamists (80x150).

The elevation of the east end of the church of St Cross which appears in *Architectural Antiquities* and also the *History of Gothic Architecture*, both by John Britton. It is dated 1 July 1818 and the artist is Charles Ferdinand Porden, the nephew of the architect William Porden. The engraver is John Le Keux (228x167).

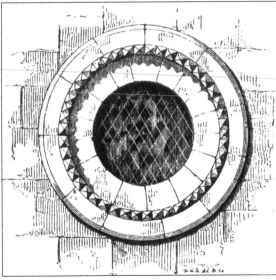

The section of the east end of the church of St Cross from the same source as the elevation on the previous page with the same artist and engraver. The date is 1 December 1818 (220x165). The circular window of the eastern gable and one of the turrets on the east end are both illustrations from the *Proceedings* of the Archaeological Institute's meeting at Winchester in 1845. The artist is Philip Henry Delamotte and the engraver John Smith Heaviside (window 48x52, turret 68x40).

Three very similar views of the church of St Cross with a section of the living accommodation. All feature lively groups of people presumably visiting residents or just admiring the buildings. At the top engraving No. 1355 by Rock and Co dated 30 March 1850 (60x90). At the centre a view by George Sidney Shepherd engraved by J. Shury and Son from Volume 3 of Robert Mudie's *Hampshire* of 1838. Are the long shadows and evening light intended to give a feel of an institution where life is gently drawing to a close? (110x150). Below an anonymous engraving published by T. Prouten of Winchester and engraved by Newman and Co. It is undated, but appears to be of a similar period to the other two (95x145).

A series of details from the church of St Cross. At the top left pointed arches drawn by Samuel Prout and engraved by John Greig from Volume 5 of the *Antiquarian and Topographical Cabinet* by James Sargant Storer and John Greig. The date is 1 December 1808 (60x55). At the top centre a view in the south transept from the *Proceedings* of the Archaeological Institute's visit to Winchester of 1845. The artist is Philip Henry Delamotte and the engraver John Smith Heaviside (95x45). At the top right something of a puzzle. This awkward double arch at the junction of the south aisle and south transept was presumably originally two doorways since blocked. It comes from the *Proceedings* of the Archaeological Institute's visit to Winchester in 1845. The artist is Philip Henry Delamotte and the engraver John Smith Heaviside (105x60). At the bottom left the west door. This illustration shows the longevity of nineteenth century pictorial work. It comes from the seventh edition of Thomas Rickman's *Gothic Architecture*, edited in 1881 by John Henry Parker forty years after Rickman's death. The original Rickman text dates back to a series of lectures published in 1817. The artist is Philip Henry Delamotte and the engraver John Smith Heaviside (67x55). Below right a window with dog toothing from Volume 16 of *Archaeologia*. The artist is John Adey Repton, the son of the landscape gardener and architect Humphrey Repton, and the engraver is James Basire. The date is 23 April 1809 (the internal view on the left 155x105, the external on the right 132x80).

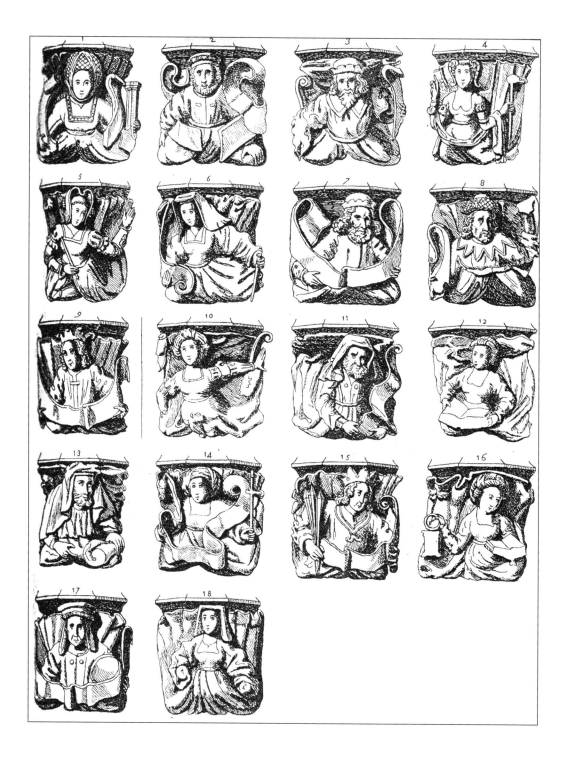

Eighteen corbel figurines thought to be holding symbols of the crucifixion from the church of St Cross and also two supporting mouldings round the west window. In addition a kneeling statue on the north side of the gateway. From Volume 2 of John Carter's *Specimens of Ancient Sculpture and Paintings*. All the illustrations are dated 1 May 1790 (corbel figurines 50x50-55, figurines supporting the mouldings 75x50, statue 75x45).

At the top left the chapel on the north side of the chancel and at the top right the font from the church of St Cross. Both illustrations are dated 1 December 1808 and comes from Volume 5 of the *Antiquarian and Topographical Cabinet* by James Sargant Storer and John Greig. The artist is Samuel Prout and the engraver Storer himself (chapel 85x60, font 65x90). At the centre right piscina and brackets in the north aisle of the choir from the *Proceedings* of the Archaeological Institute's meeting at Winchester in 1845. The artist is Philip Henry Delamotte and the engraver John Smith Heaviside (64x52). Below the consecration cross drawn by Francis Joseph Baigent dated 25 April 1864 with a publication date of 1884 (45x45). Bottom an interior view of the church of St Cross from Volume 3 of Robert Mudie's *Hampshire* of 1838. The artist is George Sidney Shepherd and the engravers J. Shury and Son (105x150)

Base of Pier, Nave.

At the top an engraving of the nave and aisles of the church of St Cross, which appears in *Architectural Antiquities* and also the *History of Gothic Architecture*, both by John Britton. It is dated 1 March 1820. The artist is Frederick Mackenzie and the engraver Samuel Rawle. It gives a much better impression of the loftiness of the church in comparison with the Shepherd view on the previous page (190x145). Below three ornamental column bases in the church of St Cross. From the *Proceedings* of the Archaeological Institute's visit to Winchester in 1845. The artist is Philip Henry Delamotte and the engraver John Smith Heaviside (each 50x40).

The south aisle of the choir looking east in the church of St Cross. This appears in *Architectural Antiquities* and also the *History of Gothic Architecture*, both by John Britton and dated 1 September 1819. The artist is Frederick Mackenzie and the engraver Samuel Rawle (200x150).

The church of St Cross looking east as altered by William Butterfield in 1864-1865, except that his original polychromatic mural decorations were subsequently removed. An anonymous drawing from the *Builder* of 28 October 1865 (270x170).

At the top left a splendid and boldly decorated lectern with an undated wooden eagle in the church of St Cross from the *Builder* of 28 October 1865 (172x122). At the top right and below pier capitals of c.1170. That at the top right is in the choir aisle and those below on the south side of the choir. They come from Edmund Sharpe's *Ornamentation of the Transitional Period of British Architecture*, undated but with a preface of 1871. The photolithography is by Whiteman and Son (choir aisle 125x55), south side of the choir 180x145).

At the top a view of part of the living accommodation at St Cross with Cardinal Beaufort's gateway and tower and the west end of the church. The artist is Thomas Hearne and the engraving comes from the *Antiquities of Great Britain* by Hearne and William Byrne originally issued in parts. It is dated 10 April 1780. In reply to a letter from John Charles Brooke, the Somerset Herald, Richard Gough wrote in February 1780 'that he had assisted Mr. Hearne, as far as I can, by the loan of the History of Winchester ...' This must presumably refer to Thomas Warton's *History & Antiquities of Winchester* of 1773 (185x255). Below left a very similar view to the one above from Volume 2 of John Milner's *History of Winchester* of 1798 to 1801. This engraving comes from the second edition of 1809. The artist is James Cave and the engraver J. Pass. It is dated 1 March 1809 (135x205). Below right the monumental brass of John de Campden on the pavement of the choir. He was warden of St Cross and the brass is dated 1382. The height of the effigy is given as 5'11" and the entire composition 7'6". From the Reverend Charles Boutell's *Monumental Brasses of England* of 1849. The artist and engraver is R.B. Utting (187x72).

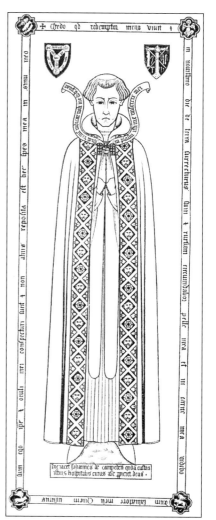

Three drawings that make an interesting comparison with the much earlier views on the previous page. At the top Cardinal Beaufort's gateway with part of the surrounding range of buildings. From the *Builder* of 18 October 1851. Although the artist's monogram is not entirely clear, it appears to be that of Orlando Jewitt (115x170). At the centre a view with a small diagram of the entire layout of St Cross and the shields in the spandrels of the gateway. It comes from Volume 1 of *Antient Domestick Architecture* by Francis Thomas Dollman and J.R. Jobbins of 1858. Dollman is also the artist (185x250). Below a drawing by Jenny Wylie dated 1908 from Volume 5 of the *Victoria County History of Hampshire* of 1912 (85x125).

At the top Cardinal Beaufort's gateway from *Old English Houses of Alms* by Sidney Heath of 1910, which is in essence a consolidation of a series of articles in the *Builder* from 11 July 1908 onwards. The artist of this detailed drawing, as for almost all the illustrations from the book, is Heath himself (210x165). Below a drawing of the gateway by Charles G. Harper from *Royal Winchester* of 1889 by the Reverend A.G. L'Estrange (115x140).

Three further views of the Beaufort gateway. The first two show the north elevation rather than the south elevation on the previous two pages. That at the top comes from the *Proceedings* of the Archaeological Institute's visit to Winchester in 1845. The artist is Philip Henry Delamotte and the engraver John Smith Heaviside (75x75). That at the centre by the artist Alfred Rimmer from his book *Ancient Streets and Homesteads of England* of 1877 (93x75), while below is a drawing showing both north and south elevations from Francis Thomas Dollman and J.R. Jobbins' *Antient Domestick Architecture* of 1858. Dollman is also the artist (215x265).

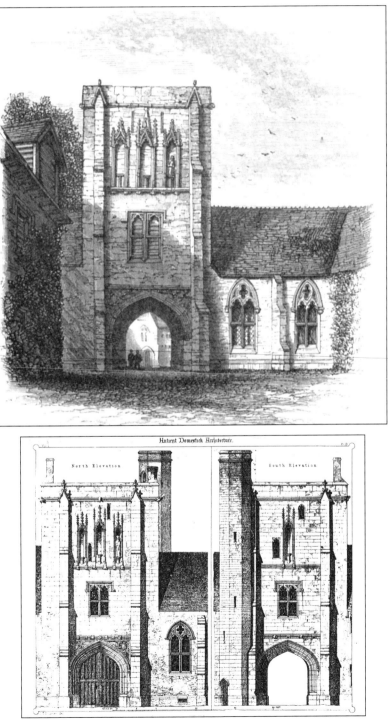

At the top the cloisters at St Cross from Volume 5 of the *Victoria County History of Hampshire* of 1912. The drawing by Jenny Wylie is dated 1908 and makes an interesting comparison with Francis Thomas Dollman's version on the next page (105x145). At the centre a view by Owen Browne Carter engraved by John Le Keux for the former's *Picturesque Memorials of Winchester* of 1830, which below left and right has been lifted almost entirely with only the people altered by the anonymous artists of the *Illustrated London News* of 13 September 1845 and the Rock and Co. engraving No. 1356 of 30 March 1850 (Carter 115x140, *Illustrated London News* 110x115, Rock and Co. 60x85).

Two further illustrations from Francis Thomas Dollman and J.R. Jobbins' *Antient Domestick Architecture* of 1858, one of the ambulatory and the other of the front and back of the living accommodation, both with copious detailing. The artist is Dollman himself (ambulatory 210x265, living accommodation 220x260).

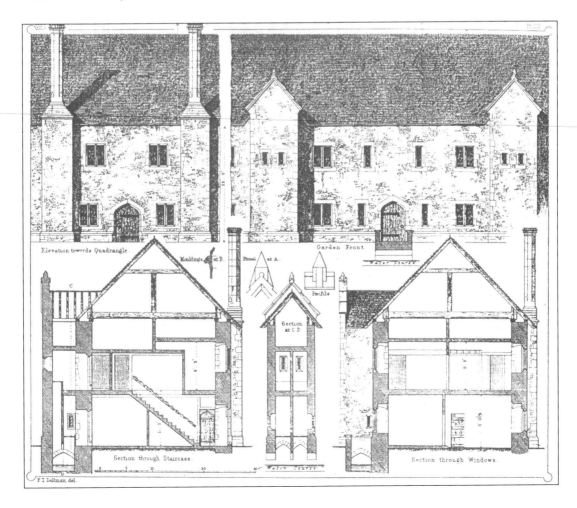

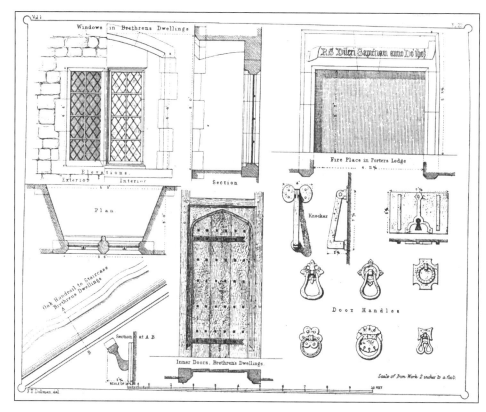

More details of the living accommodation and also of the refectory at St Cross. Both illustrations are from Francis Thomas Dollman and J.R. Jobbins' *Antient Domestick Architecture* of 1858. The artist is Dollman himself (whole plate of living accommodation details 210x255, whole plate of refectory details 210x280).

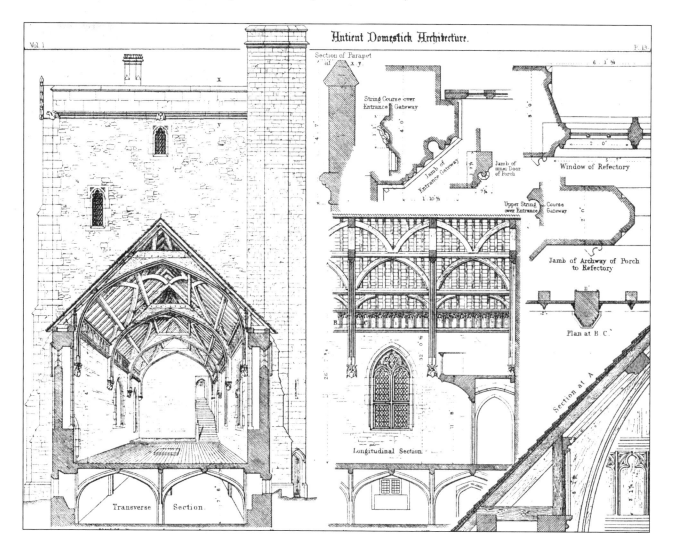

Three views of the refectory at St Cross. At the top a draw-
ing by Owen Browne Carter engraved by John Le Keux from
Carter's *Picturesque Memorials of Winchester* of 1830.
Below left an anonymous engraving from the *Illustrated
London News* of 13 September 1845, showing antiquarian
gentlemen making an inspection during the meeting of the
Archaeological Institute in Winchester. Their well clothed
and prosperous air makes a decided contrast with the old men
in Carter's drawing. Below right a sketch by Arthur Leslie
Collins from Volume 5 of the *Victoria Country History of
Hampshire* of 1912 (Carter 120x135, *Illustrated London
News* 110x115, Collins 135x100).

Two further views of the refectory at St Cross, both from the other end compared with those on the previous page. That above is a drawing by William Henry Bartlett engraved by Edward John Roberts for Volume 1 of Bernard Bolingbroke Woodward's *General History of Hampshire* of 1861 to 1869. Two of the residents seem to be warming themselves by an open fire while others are eating a meal (125x165). Left a sketch by Sidney Heath from his work *Old English Houses of Alms* of 1910 (200x150).

ACKNOWLEDGEMENTS

In writing a work of this kind it is necessary to seek the advice, and guidance of a large number of people and I would like to acknowledge with grateful thanks help from the following people and institutions; the Society of Antiquaries for permission to reproduce material and especially its Librarian Bernard Nurse and his staff for chasing material often out of distant and obscure parts of the Society's premises; the staffs of the London Library, the RIBA Library and the local history section of the Hampshire County Library at Winchester; Robin Freeman for specialist knowledge on Owen Browne Carter; Christopher Currie, the General Editor of the *Victoria History of the Counties of England*, also for permission to reproduce material; Dr Christopher Wakeling for information on the architectural practice of Poulton and Woodman; my old friends Alison and Tony Latcham for allowing me to stay with them in Winchester; my wife Marion for her expert knowledge as an architectural historian and also as a photographer in producing large numbers of transparencies for many of the illustrations; Steven Pugsley and his staff at Halsgrove Publishing for encouragement through the foothills of compilation; Mark Oaten M.P. for Winchester for writing the Foreword; and finally and not least, all those many artists and engravers, long since gathered to their ancestors, who have made this book possible. If I had to make the invidious choice of one individual to stand for all the rest it would be John Le Keux, whose name appears so frequently in these pages and about whom John Britton wrote, 'No English engraver has done more to enhance the fame of his art and give peculiar interest and value to that branch which he professed and practised for so many years'.

A yolly was Winchester College slang for a postchaise which was usually yellow, and this view of scholars off for the hols makes a fitting illustration for the author to take leave of his readers. It comes from Robert Blachford Mansfield's *School Life at Winchester College* of 1863. Although the sketch is unsigned, it is presumably by the unfortunate Henry Garland, whom Mansfield takes to task twice in his book, the second time in the glossary of slang section with the words, 'The few woodcuts interspersed through the Glossary are not of such faithful representations as the author could have wished. However, they serve in some measure to explain the various colloquialisms'. As a great oarsman and pioneer of English golf, Mansfield obviously thought artists were effete and highly dubious characters (55x95).

SUGGESTIONS
FOR FURTHER READING

Alarge number of books and periodicals are mentioned in the body of the text and it seems pointless merely to list them again in this section. Readers will make their own judgments about whether they wish to consult them further and in any event they naturally vary widely in value, accuracy and usefulness. For biographical information of a general nature the *Dictionary of National Biography* and *Who Was Who* are essential. More specialist works I have found useful are Simon Houfe's *Dictionary of Nineteenth Century Book Illustrators* (revised edition 1996) and Ronald Russell's *Guide to Topographical Prints* (1979), but above all Bernard Adams' *London Illustrated 1604-1851* (1983). Although this outstanding work of scholarship is primarily concerned with illustrations of the Capital, it contains detailed information about a host of authors, publishers and illustrators of books covering country-wide geographical areas, but with some London material, as well as publications about London alone.

For early architects, Michael Hicks' *Who's Who in Late Medieval England 1272-1485* (1991) and John Harvey's *English Medieval Architects – A Biographical Dictionary* (1984) are useful. For later architects Sir Howard Colvin's *Dictionary of British Architects 1600-1840* (third edition 1995) is indispensable and the *Dictionary of British Architects 1834-1900* (1993) brings the story up to the end of the nineteenth century. For detailed architectural information about Winchester the *Hampshire* volume of the Buildings of England series edited by Sir Nikolaus Pevsner and David Lloyd (1967) is still essential reading and a revised edition is currently being researched.

The massive work entitled *Winchester Studies* edited by Martin Biddle from 1976 onwards and has resulted so far in seven volumes throwing a truly dazzling searchlight on the development of the medieval City and is required reading for any proper understanding of the period. Two general works still of value are W. Lloyd Woodland's *Story of Winchester* in the medieval towns series (1932) and Brian Vesey Fitzgerald's *Winchester* (1953). For those interested in Wykeham and Wynford's building work outside Winchester and Oxford, the first two volumes of the *King's Works* (1963) provide a detailed analysis and Volume 7 of the *Wren Society* (1930) covers the Winchester Royal Palace, while the Bankside Volume (No 22) of the *Survey of London* (1950) has the best account of Winchester Palace.

For the Cathedral by far the most rewarding survey is *Winchester Cathedral 1093-1993* (1993) edited by John Crook, which is a series of contributions by subject experts on differing aspects of the building. *Winchester Cathedral 1074-1979* (1979) by Frederick Bussby has a more straightforward chronological approach and goes into a great deal of interesting material. John Crook is also the author of a *History of Pilgrim's School*.

For the College *Winchester College* (1981) by the present Headmaster, James Sabben-Clare, casts a naturally sympathetic eye over its six-hundred-year history, but also does not pull any punches when it comes to the less endearing aspects and episodes of the past. Four other works of note all also entitled *Winchester College* deserve attention. The study of 1926 by the College Archaeological Society is full of detail, as also is that by Canon J. de Frith (1949 - revised edition 1961). Christopher Hawkes' book (1933) is slighter, but is accompanied by a series of magnificent photographs by a staff member of *Country Life*. The compilation of fifteen essays by a number of scholars edited by Roger Custance (1983) covers many intriguing and often controversial aspects of life during the College's history.

For St Cross Peter Hopewell's *St Cross – England's Oldest Almshouse* (1995) is a general survey and Yoshio Kusaba's *Architectural History of the Church of St Cross* (1983) is a detailed analysis of the building. Robin Freeman's *Art and Architecture of Owen Browne Carter* (1991) and Harry Carter's *Orlando Jewitt* (1962) cover the life and work of two of the important topographical artists who feature largely in this work. *A History of King Alfred's College Winchester* (1981) by Martial Rose and a *History of the Royal Hampshire County Hospital* (1986) by Barbara Carpenter Turner are two books covering important institutions in the City and the latter author is also responsible among other productions for *St Johns Winchester Charity* and a *History of Winchester* (revised edition 1992).